# Contributions to Finance and Accounting

The book series 'Contributions to Finance and Accounting' features the latest research from research areas like financial management, investment, capital markets, financial institutions, FinTech and financial innovation, accounting methods and standards, reporting, and corporate governance, among others. Books published in this series are primarily monographs and edited volumes that present new research results, both theoretical and empirical, on a clearly defined topic. All books are published in print and digital formats and disseminated globally.

More information about this series at https://link.springer.com/bookseries/16616

Bruno Buchetti • Alessandro Santoni

# Corporate Governance in the Banking Sector

## Theory, Supervision, ESG and Real Banking Failures

Springer

Bruno Buchetti
University of Padua
Padua, Italy

Alessandro Santoni
Frankfurt, Hessen, Germany

ISSN 2730-6038 ISSN 2730-6046 (electronic)
Contributions to Finance and Accounting
ISBN 978-3-030-97574-6 ISBN 978-3-030-97575-3 (eBook)
https://doi.org/10.1007/978-3-030-97575-3



This Springer imprint is published by the registered company Springer Nature Switzerland AG
The registered company address is: Gewerbestrasse 11, 6330 Cham, Switzerland

*This book is dedicated to my Dad and my Mom who are an example of family, dedication and unconditional love.—Alessandro Santoni*
*This book is dedicated to my grandfather Adino Bruno Buchetti.—Bruno Buchetti*

# Authors' Comment

The authors' knowledge on the subject does not derive uniquely from academic background but also from the professional experience on the subject on primary Institutions as Goldman Sachs, Credit Suisse, European Central Bank (ECB), and International Monetary Fund (IMF).[1]

---

[1] **Disclaimer**: This book should not be reported as representing the views of these institutions. The views expressed are those of the authors and do not necessarily reflect those of these organizations.

---

The original version of this book was revised: city name updated for Bruno Buchetti. The correction to this book can be found at https://doi.org/10.1007/978-3-030-97575-3_7

# Acknowledgements

We are especially grateful to Federico Salerno, Arun Kelshiker. Konstantinos Koryllos, Valentina Rapalino, Samuele Crosetti for their valuable support.

# Introduction

In the past 20 years, largely due to financial scandals, attention toward bank corporate governance (CG) processes has increased significantly, accompanied by a renewed interest in the analysis of its effectiveness and its impact on risk appetite and performance. This book aims to clarify and extend the role and importance of an efficient CG system within the banking sector. It looks at CG constructs through an innovative lens; in fact, it connects CG theory (proposing the existence of two new agency costs in the banking sector) with global banking regulation, empirical research results (discussing the main findings), and real cases of CG failures in the banking context. The main goal of this book is to clarify the principal characteristics of CG, investigating how good CG practices can become a tool for better protecting shareholders, stakeholders, citizens, and the economy in general.

In Chap. 1, we clarify the meaning of "corporate governance." We focus on the main difficulties that regulators, practitioners, and the general public face when discussing CG topics. We find that some specific features of CG exacerbate this challenge, making it problematic to standardize CG concepts. For example, we find that CG regulation is a very recent phenomenon all over the world, and in the banking sector, this is even more true. Second, we highlight how CG looks at social relations between people, making it very difficult to measure, and above all, operationalize[2] CG constructs. Third, we show that when the ownership structures of firms and banks are different, the CG characteristics and goals change. Fourth, we find that CG models differ according to the diverse forms of capitalism, which means that generalizing CG results is very dangerous; this is due to the very high risk of comparing settings that, by definition, are different from each other and thus need a different regulation and supervision.

[2]"Operationalization" is the process of strictly defining "abstract concepts" into measurable observations (e.g., gender diversity -> operationalization (in the corporate governance area) -> percentage of female directors on the board)

Finally, we examine the main definitions of CG with a focus on the banking sector.

In Chap. 2, we explain the main CG theories. We start with the agency theory and we investigate how agency costs change in the banking context. For the first time, these new agency costs are identified, analyzed, and above all we propose some mechanisms to reduce them. After we describe and compare the shareholders' and stakeholders' theories. Finally, we describe the other most relevant CG theories, i.e. the Stewardship Theory, the Resource Dependency Theory (RDT), the Shareholders Theory, the Stakeholders Theory, the Resource Based View Theory (RBV), and the Upper Echelons Theory (UET).

In Chap. 3, we investigate how researchers all over the world are trying to disentangle CG constructs in the banking context. We scrutinize the main articles published in the years 2000–2020 which investigate corporate governance in the banking sector (CGBS) topics, and we identify the most studied areas, i.e. risk appetite and risk management, board diversity, ownership structure, role of CEO, compensation, Islamic banking systems, CSR and environmental, social, and corporate governance (ESG) indicators, and political connections. We find the following: (a) increasing the proportion of independent directors might amplify the risk appetite of banks (this is particularly true in large and international banks, when there is a one-tier board, and if independent directors have financial expertise); (b) CEO-duality, usually considered a signal of poor CG quality, might actually reduce (but not always) the risk appetite of banks; (c) in China and in the USA, increasing the proportion of women sitting on the board seems to reduce the risk appetite of banks, while in Europe, there are mixed or negative results; (d) gender diversity generally improves the level of CSR disclosure; (e) gender diversity appears to mitigate the excessive compensation of directors; (f) the presence of foreign shareholders might potentially improve the performance of banks; (g) the existence of foreign shareholders seems to have a positive impact on the level of CSR disclosure; (h) a concentrated ownership structure might increase the risk appetite of banks; and (i) a concentrated ownership structure appears to mitigate the excessive compensation of directors.

In Chap. 4, we review the literature on the relationship between bank governance and stock performance. Academic analysis concludes there are various and very diverse findings on several governance parameters that might affect stock performance of companies. We highlighted four relations between stock prices and ownership concentration, board of directors, executive compensation, and finally executive management.

If the empirical analysis testify that Governance has an undoubtful impact on stock price, we then examine how this correlation is used by the investment industry. On this aspects, ESG[3] indexes, that incorporate Governance aspects as key criteria, are becoming increasingly popular benchmarks. We investigated the nature of the five blocks composing the pillars of the Governance criteria within the main ESG

[3]Environmental, social, and corporate governance.

indexes. They are Board effectiveness, Stakeholder Governance, Governance Ethics, Governance disclosure, and Shareholders rights. Each of these provisions has several sub-provisions. The rational of their inclusion in the indexes laid mainly on the empirical evidence of their relevance. There is now a consolidated literature highlighting the importance of these factors. The attention to Governance factors also activated a significant amount of regulation on the topic. Regulatory framework infrastructure is now vast. However, governance scandals have not diminished suggesting that even if the governance infrastructure was adequate, the board and management behavior sometimes was inadequate. A perfect infrastructure could help to maintain a good governance but, after all, Banks are made by human being with their biases.

Similarly, Board decision-making process and CEOs biases have been at the center of academic literature studies on behavioral economics following the financial crisis in the first decade of 2000. We described some of the most common irrational beliefs or behavior that can unconsciously influence Board and CEOs decision-making process. From the Board side, we highlighted four concepts as bounded rationality, *problemistic* search, the routinization of decision-making in standard operating procedures, and the political bargaining. From the CEOs side, we highlighted overconfidence together with present-biased preferences, WACC fallacy, conservatism bias, and representativeness heuristic.

In Chap. 5, we describe how a charismatic CEOs ideally can influence financial fundamentals and market performances leveraging on reputation, track record, and confidence. This halo effect can impact major corporate stakeholders as analysts and fund managers leveraging on their behavioral bias. This connection can sometime transform into a vicious circle bringing to dramatic consequences. We investigate the Enron case along with the UK Banks scandals in 2008 as examples on how the top-managers' behavior can influence the decision-making process and how this could interrelate with market participants as analysts and fund managers. These examples show how CEOs could successfully capture the most educated among the stakeholders of the market environment creating a toxic environment that generates failures of enormous dimensions.

The relevance of behavioral bias in the decision-making process and their impacts become such a relevant aspect of the organization that some Banking Supervisors as DNB[4], FSA, and APRA[5] decided to include aspects of behavior and culture into their supervisory approach.

A basic principle for that is that failures and fraud often are preceded by ineffective behavior. As such, it seems reasonable to pay attention to behavior as a financial supervisor. Focusing on behavior would allow Supervisors to proactively identifying and "intercepting" ineffective behavior at an early stage preventing their conversion into financial problems.

---

[4] Supervision of Behavior and Culture: Foundations, Practice and Future Developments. 2015

[5] http://www.apra.gov.au/CrossIndustry/Documents/161018-Information-Paper-Risk-Culture.pdf

In Chap. 6, we analyzed some of the most famous bankruptcies revealing severe inadequacies both in internal management and in the role of the board in overseeing risk management control functions. We put particularly emphasis on the analysis of the governance failures and their root causes. From the enormous amount of literature written on these scandals, we particularly focused on the micro governance issues that created the opportunity to bypass internal controls.

It was 1:45 in the morning of the 15th of September 2008 when Lehman Brothers filed bankruptcy. The largest proceeding ever, something that nearly caused a collapse of the world's financial system. Lehman bankruptcy was analyzed and explained with several technical reasons mainly focusing on excessive leverage and excessive credit risk among others. It is undisputable however that the trigger that dragged Lehman into bankruptcy was its inability to keep confidence of its counterparties and as a consequence it runs short of liquidity. We analyzed the Governance aspect of this spectacular default showing failure of government oversight, bad management decision till intentional balance sheet manipulation.

The bankruptcy of BCCI (Bank of Credit and Commerce International) is considered as one of the greatest financial disasters of the last century. Founded in 1972 by a Pakistani banker, the BCCI had an exponential growth, so much so that in ten years it became the seventh bank in the world for assets. The financial failure of the BCCI was peculiar in the history of bank failures as it develops in parallel with the development of the Bank. The magnitude of loophole in internal and external controls (at all levels) makes the BCCI bankruptcy a case study for corporate governance failure.

The bankruptcy of the German Bank Bankhaus Herstatt is considered, due to the ramifications of its impacts, despite its small size, as the determining factor that prompted the central bank governors of the ten most industrialized countries to launch the Banking Supervision Committee (Basel Committee). Herstatt failure provides an illustration of the consequences of poor oversight by the supervisors, poor internal governance as well as the limitation of market self-regulation[6].

Finally, we examined two among the most famous cases of rogue trader scandals i.e. involving Societe Generale and UBS in 2008 and 2011 respectively. Francois Brochet[7] wrote that the Societe Generale case, illustrates the tension/balance that firms with complex and risky business models must consider in designing their internal controls. It describes the environment in which a derivatives trader engaged in massive directional positions on major European stocks and indexes without being detected for over a year. Just three years after the this scandal, a very similar incident hit UBS credibility. The aim is not to describe the frauds per se but rather highlights the governance holes described by the investigations.

---

[6]Emmanuel Mourlon-Druol "'Trust is good, control is better': The 1974 Herstatt Bank Crisis and its Implications for International Regulatory Reform Adam Smith Business School, University of Glasgow, Glasgow" UK https://www.tandfonline.com/doi/full/10.1080/00076791.2014.950956

[7]Brochet, Francois. "Societe Generale (A): The Jerome Kerviel Affair." Harvard Business School Case 110-029, October 2009. (Revised April 2010.)

# Contents

# About the Authors

**Bruno Buchetti** is a contract Professor of Corporate Governance and Management at the University of Padua (Italy).

He worked at the European Central Bank (Frankfurt am Main, Germany) as a Supervision Analyst. He covered two divisions: "Micro-prudential Supervision I" and "COI—Centralized On-Site Inspections."

He also worked in Credit Suisse (Zurich, Switzerland) as an Analyst (banking inspector).

He received his Ph.D. in Management and Innovation from the UCSC University (Milan, Italy). He holds a BSc in Economics and Business Administration and a MSc in Banking and Finance summa cum laude. During his MSc, thanks to a scholarship for academic merit, he participated in an exchange program at Stanford University (USA—California).

His research has been published in refereed international journals including "The Journal of Management and Governance" and the "Journal of Accounting and Public Policy." He is the author of "*Corporate Governance and Firm Value in Italy: How Directors and Board* Members Matter" published in 2021 (Springer Nature).

His main research interests are focused on corporate governance, financial accounting and banking.

**Alessandro Santoni** is working for the International Monetary Fund (IMF) and was previously the European Central Bank (ECB) manager responsible for Onsite Inspection and previously for Banks Crisis Management Interventions. He was involved in several banking crises, insolvency proceedings, and resolution measures. He also contributed to developing the post-crisis financial safety net in the EU and Emerging markets. Previously he worked in the Banking industry for more than 15 years in Commercial Banks as BMPS and Investments Banks as Goldman Sachs. He has a Ph.D. from the University of Siena, Master in International Economics from SDA Bocconi, and an EMBA from Columbia University, London Business

School and Hong Kong University. He has three degrees in Economics, History, and Political Science from the University of Siena. He is Certified Financial Crime Specialist (CFCS) and AML Specialist (CAMS). He teaches Risk Management, Financial Crimes at the Cass University of London and the Frankfurt School of Management. He is the author of several academic papers and books.

# Chapter 1
# The Meaning of Corporate Governance and its Role in the Banking Sector

## 1.1 Why Is CG Difficult to Describe and Regulate?

For many years, CG was considered a relevant topic merely for researchers and board directors. Practitioners, consultants, and the general public thought the CG was something intangible and difficult to measure and describe. The theories that aimed to define the relevance of CG and its related risks have been misunderstood or misinterpreted many times by the same officials responsible for monitoring and supervising the market. Therefore, directors' behaviors were rarely supervised, which generated huge risks for the entire economy. We will see this aspect in Chap. 6, which examines the largest bank failures across the world through a CG lens.

However, questions arise, such as why did this happen? Why is it so complicated to investigate and regulate how firms and banks govern themselves?

The authors have identified the following four main reasons:

I. CG regulation is recent and is usually based on the "comply-or-explain" mechanism.
II. CG looks at and measures social relationships between people.
III. CG changes when the ownership structure is different.
IV. CG differs according to the diverse forms of capitalism that are embraced.

### *1.1.1 CG Regulation Is Recently a Topic that Is Mainly Based on the "Comply-or-Explain" Mechanism*

When we tried to identify the first publication about CG, we found the "Financial Aspects of Corporate Governance Report" (also called Cadbury Report) published in 1992 in the UK. This report was issued after a series of major corporate scandals correlated with governance failures. It was the first detailed guidance on CG and



B. Buchetti, A. Santoni, *Corporate Governance in the Banking Sector*, Contributions to Finance and Accounting, https://doi.org/10.1007/978-3-030-97575-3_1

defined a series of recommendations for UK listed companies. The three main recommendations were as follows: (a) the chief executive officer (CEO) should not also be the chairman of the company (also called CEO duality); (b) the company should appoint a minimum of three nonexecutive directors, and two of them should not have ties with any executive (now called independent directors); and (c) the audit committee for the board of directors (BODs) should only be composed of nonexecutive directors. The code also provided the first definition of CG.[1] In 2003, the code was combined with the Greenbury Report and took the name of "Combined Code on Corporate Governance." It was revised after the Enron scandal and subsequently updated in June 2006 and June 2008. Today, the code is called the "UK Corporate Governance Code" (2018) and sets out several best practices and principles of good governance for companies listed on the London Stock Exchange. Despite the recommendations and principles defined in the report, *they are not compulsory*. The Financial Reporting Council (FRC)[2] asks companies to "comply or explain," that is, either apply the code or explain why they do not. This "comply-or-explain" method is normally adopted for all CG codes. In fact, in the CG setting, it is less common to find laws that directly enforce companies or banks to change or modify their CG structure and composition. However, this nonmandatory system may generate opportunistic behaviors. Fortunately, financial investors in today's economy are more concerned about CG aspects and valuing good CG practices. After the Cadbury Report in 1992, CG codes started to proliferate all over the world. For example, in Europe, at the end of 1990s, 15 countries had issued their own CG codes.

The first supranational CG guidelines are even more recent; in 1999, the Organisation for Economic Co-operation and Development (OECD) issued a set of guidelines and CG standards to help governments improve the CG regulatory frameworks in their countries. The guidelines referred to both corporations and banking institutions but were not binding. They were revised in 2004 after the WorldCom, Enron, and Parmalat failures.

However, it is only because of the Basel Committee on Banking Supervision (BCBS)[3] in 1999—with the "Enhancing Corporate Governance for Banking Organizations"—that the first international CG guidance for the banking sector was introduced. These CG principles were modernized in 2006 and 2010, and in 2015, the BCBS issued the "Corporate governance principles for banks." This revised guidance emphasizes the pivotal role of effective CG for the sound and safe

[1] See Sect. 1.2.

[2] The FRC is the UK's regulator for the actuarial, accounting, and audit professions; it is also responsible for CG in the UK.

[3] The Basel Committee on Banking Supervision was established by a number of central bank governors. From the BCBS website: "The Basel Committee on Banking Supervision (BCBS) is the primary global standard setter for the prudential regulation of banks and provides a forum for regular cooperation on banking supervisory matters" (https://www.bis.org/bcbs/ *last accessed 31.12.2021*).

**Table 1.1** CG codes for banks

| Setting | Regulator | First introduction |
|---|---|---|
| International | Basel Committee | 1999 |
| Singapore | Monetary Authority of Singapore | 2005 |
| Nigeria | The Central Bank of Nigeria | 2006 |
| Italy | Bank of Italy | 2008 |
| Qatar | Qatar Central Bank | 2008 |
| Yemen | Central Bank of Yemen | 2008 |
| Jordan | Central Bank of Jordan | 2008 |
| UK | HM Treasury | 2009 |
| Netherlands | Nederlandse Vereniging van Banken | 2009 |
| Georgia | Association of Banks of Georgia | 2009 |
| Ireland | Central Bank of Ireland | 2010 |
| Iraq | Central Bank of Iraq | 2018 |
| Ghana | Bank of Ghana | 2018 |
| UAE | Central Bank of the UAE | 2019 |

Source: Authors constructed using ECGI website (European Corporate Governance Institute (ECGI): https://ecgi.global/) and other multiple sources

functioning of banks. Subsequently, the BCBS issued several different reports addressing questions about the role of CG in the banking sector.

Why is CG regulation in the banking sector at this early stage?

Because until the 2008 financial crisis, regulators and the general public were not conscious of the risks generated by poorly managed board of directors to the global economy!

Now we know this very well, but until 10 years ago, it was considered very dangerous to regulate or even discuss governance matters in this area. Today is clear the connection between bad governance and the risk of banks' failures and potential systemic risk. About this aspect, in 2009, the OECD supported the idea that bad CG practices were one of the main factors that may have contributed to the Great Financial Crisis:

> ... the financial crisis can be to an important extent attributed to failures and weaknesses in corporate governance arrangements which did not serve their purpose to safeguard against excessive risk taking in a number of financial services companies. Kirkpatrick OECD (2009)

Hence, the financial crisis was the turning point that determined the explosion of ad hoc CG codes for banks all around the world. We can see this clearly in Table 1.1, where the main CG codes for banks are sorted by date. We can observe that most CG codes for banks were issued only during (or after) the Great Financial Crisis in 2008. It is important to point out that these codes are different from the CG codes issued in these countries (usually applicable to listed companies); we can say that they are ad hoc regulations typically issued from the national central banks and applicable only at bank level. We can observe, as we could expect, that banks require specific CG regulation.

**Table 1.2** CG regulation in bank and nonbank companies

| CG | CG in corporations | CG in banking | Potential solutions and/or next steps |
|---|---|---|---|
| CG regulations and related guidelines are a recent topic | Important problem | Very important problem (very recent regulation) | Where CG failures are evident and repeated over time, move from a "comply-or-explain approach" typical of CG codes to a mandatory approach, that is, issuing ad hoc regulations |

Source: Authors constructed

Table 1.2 compares how these recent CG regulations make difficult to clarify the CG construct in bank and nonbank companies and suggests possible solutions.

### *1.1.2 CG Looks at and Measures Social Relationships between People*

CG looks at social relationships between people, and we know that measuring, regulating, and explaining social elements can be extremely difficult and dangerous. In fact, there is always the risk of missing relevant facts that you cannot identify simply by looking at data or behaviors inside the board (e.g., are the directors' decisions really taken during the board meetings or at the golf club?).

In academia, there are two main methods of investigating CG topics: the quantitative approach that mainly utilizes archival data and embraces the agency theory as its theoretical background (Hambrick et al. 2008; Dalton et al. 2007; Daily et al. 2003) and the "qualitative approach," which is usually based on a comparison of multiple case studies generally augmented by conducting interviews, surveys, focus groups, or using secondary archival data.

Using the quantitative approach, you can either look at data about the BOD as a single entity or you can investigate specific directors' characteristics. For example, if you decide to investigate directors' characteristics, you can look at their gender (Mazzotta and Ferraro 2020; Cardillo et al. 2021; Proença et al. 2020; Kusi et al. 2018; Dong et al. 2017; Nguyen et al. 2015; Gregory-Smith et al. 2014; Liu et al. 2014; Ahern and Dittmar 2012; Adams and Ferreira 2009) and social aspects, like ethnicity and age (Shukeri et al. 2012; Carter et al. 2010; Darmadi 2010, Miller 2009), or you can refer to multidimensional indexes (Buchetti 2021; Bernile et al. 2018; Anderson et al. 2011). These indexes usually cover directors' specific qualities, for example, previous experience in important industries (e.g., banks, law firms, consulting companies, accounting, and audit firms), connections with other companies (are they a director or CEO of another company?), members of relevant institutions (e.g., universities or political parties), or international corporates (Rossignoli et al. 2021).

Instead, if you look at the board as a singular entity, you can investigate the board size (Pfeffer 1972), the number of executive or nonexecutive directors (Pass 2004; Clifford and Evans 1997), the role of the independent directors (Clarke 2007; Petra 2005), the number of directors appointed from minority shareholders (Kim et al. 2007), the frequency of BOD meetings (Vafeas 1999), the presence of the Lead Independent Director (Masulis and Mobbs 2014), etc.

Subsequently, researchers investigate if these elements affect different firms' features, for example, the performance (Bhagat and Bolton 2008), the strategy (Pugliese et al. 2009), the level of social responsibility (Jo and Harjoto 2011; Jamali et al. 2008; Smith et al. 2006; Ferreira 2010), the average compensation (Brick et al. 2006), the financial structure (Ferreira 2010), and the level of internationalization (Barroso et al. 2011).

In the banking environment,[4] governance features are usually linked to risk appetite (Basiruddin and Ahmed 2020; Dong et al. 2017; Neifar and Jarboui et al. 2018; De Vita and Luo 2018; Vallascas et al. 2017), performance (Belkhir 2009), compensation (Byrd et al. 2010; Angbazo 1997), corporate social responsibility (CSR) disclosure (Jizi et al. 2014), the takeover market (Brickley and James 1987), and impact on environmental, social, and corporate governance (ESG) performance (Birindelli et al. 2018). In Table 1.3, the main CG constructs investigated in literature and their relation with firms' and banks' characteristics are reported.

Alternatively, you can investigate the relationships within the BOD by recording a board meeting to identify and describe specific common patterns (see, for example, Bezemer et al. (2014)), or you can simply interview board members. This method is called the qualitative approach, which is less common (McNulty et al. 2013; Turley and Zaman 2004) but aims to identify common behaviors among directors and describe board dynamics.

The qualitative approach is even less common in the banking sector. Only 4% of articles published in scientific journals that belong to the Q1 Scimago ranking utilize the qualitative approach (see Chap. 3).

Table 1.4 shows how measuring CG social aspects can make difficult to clarify the CG concept in bank and nonbank companies and suggests possible solutions.

### *1.1.3 CG Structure and Goals Change when the Ownership Structure Is Different*

The CG perimeter changes according to the distinctive aims pursued by the different types of owners of a company (Sur et al. 2013; Bartholomeusz and Tanewski 2006). In fact, two important questions in clarifying the role of the BOD are as follows: who is the owner of the company and what are its goals? For example, the roles and goals

[4] Please refer to Chaps. 3 and 4 to see the latest research on CG in the banking sector.

**Table 1.3** Main CG relations studied in companies and banks

| CG—Directors' characteristics | CG—Board characteristics | CG—Ownership structure | Impact on firms | Impact on banks (from Chap. 3) |
|---|---|---|---|---|
| * Age<br>* Gender<br>* Education<br>* Work experiences<br>* Connections with other companies<br>* Connections with political parties | * Board size<br>* The proportion of independent directors<br>* Committee (presence and characteristics)<br>* Proportion of executive and nonexecutive members<br>* Proportion of directors appointed by minority lists<br>* Frequency of the meetings<br>* The presence of the Lead Independent Director<br>* CEO power (usually CEO duality) | * Concentrated vs. dispersed<br>* Type of ownership structure: family, institutional, foreign, governmental, etc. | * Performance<br>* Compensation<br>* Accounting quality<br>* CSR<br>* Disclosure<br>* Strategy<br>* Internationalization<br>* M&A | * Risk appetite<br>* Performance<br>* Accounting quality<br>* CSR & ESG<br>* Disclosure<br>* Compensation<br>* M&A<br>* Cost-efficiency<br>* Islamic banks' peculiarities |

Source: Authors constructed

**Table 1.4** Measuring social aspects in bank and nonbank companies

| CG | CG in corporations | CG in banking | Potential solutions and/or next steps |
|---|---|---|---|
| CG looks at directors' attributes, social aspects, and board characteristics. These elements are very difficult to measure, evaluate, and regulate | Very important problem | Very important problem | (a) Increase the amount of research that utilizes a qualitative approach as this area is too small<br>(b) When regulators decide to issue new CG laws and codes, they should be very careful because they are regulating social aspects that are very difficult to operationalize and measure |

Source: Authors constructed

of board members change if the owner is a private equity fund, a family, the State, or a corporate parent.

In family-controlled firms,[5] the BOD's goal is to preserve the family's wealth[6] (Berrone et al. 2012). Family members sitting on the BOD can also make choices that could be detrimental in terms of maximizing the company's value[7] if these choices preserve the family endowment (Berrone et al. 2012); for example, family members could extract benefits from the company against minority shareholders, causing damage to them[8] (Lubatkin et al. 2005; Schulze et al. 2001). In these firms, the executive directors or the CEO are usually family members, so their role is not monitoring managers' behavior as this would happen when there is a widely dispersed ownership structure. Family-controlled firms are characterized by a highly concentrated ownership structure where outside directors (nonfamily directors) are appointed according to their expertise and contribution of resources to the company (Sur et al. 2013; Buchetti 2021). In fact, family members can lack the technical or professional expertise that is needed for the company's success.

If the owner is a private equity fund, the directors' goal will be to increase the company's short-term value to sell the company for a higher price than was paid. In this book, the perimeter will be the financial sector, particularly the BOD in banks. The ownership structure of a bank can be different, and the main shareholders usually comprise large foundations, other banks, foreign investors, individuals or

[5]Family-controlled firms are the most common for organizations in today's economy (La porta et al. 1999).

[6]This wealth in family firms literature is also called "socioemotional wealth" (please refer to Gómez-Mejía et al. (2007) and Berrone et al. (2012)).

[7]This does not mean that family firms underperform compared to other companies; at the opposite, many studies find that family firms generally outperform nonfamily firms under certain conditions (Anderson and Reeb 2003; Lee 2006; Villalonga and Amit 2006; Van Essen et al. 2015).

[8]For example, a family that holds the 51% of shares can decide to purchase a house for the son of the owner. These opportunistic behaviors are also called "private benefits of control."

**Table 1.5** The role of the ownership structure in bank and nonbank CG

| CG | CG in corporations | CG in banking | Potential solutions and/or next steps |
|---|---|---|---|
| The CG perimeter **changes according to the distinctive aims pursued by the different types of owners of a company** | Very important problem | Important problem | (a) Always wonder who the owner is |

Source: Authors constructed

families, and the State. We have to remember that in banks, there is a more defined scope than in other sectors. The Basel Committee on Banking Supervision gives a clear definition on the main goals of CG in the banking system and outlines banking supervision in its guidelines. The Corporate Governance Principle for Banks (2015) defines the scope of CG in a bank as "The primary objective of corporate governance should be safeguarding stakeholders' interest in conformity with public interest on a sustainable basis. Among stakeholders, particularly with respect to retail banks, shareholders' interest would be secondary to depositors' interest." In this case the role of the owners (i.e., the shareholders) is secondary to a specific stakeholder (i.e., the depositors). We can observe that the goals persued by the different owners are more restricted in the banking indutry making CG objectives clearer. We will return to this definition in Chap. 2.

Table 1.5 reports how the different ownership structures affect the CG constructs in companies and banks.

### *1.1.4 CG Differs According to the Diverse Forms of Capitalism that Are Embraced*

The literature describes three different CG models, that is, the Anglo-American model, the Continental European model, and the Japanese model. These existing models are modified and customized according to nations' political, social, economic, and legal values.[9] These aspects affect BODs: (a) composition, (b) aims, and (c) structure.

To provide an example of this, the Anglo-American model of CG (also called the Anglo-Saxon approach) existing in the United States, UK, Canada, Australia, India, and the commonwealth countries tends to accentuate the interests of the shareholders, that is, the company's only duty is to maximize shareholder value (so-called shareholder's model or "shareholder's view"[10]). In this context, there are a few major block holdings but mostly dispersed shareholdings. The legislation is also usually hostile to concentration, and this is especially true in the banking system. In this environment, banks are simply considered "credit providers," and the

[9] All these elements will be here described as "different forms of capitalism."

[10] In Chap. 2, the "stakeholders' and shareholders' theory" will be scrutinized.

system is oriented toward the stock market (i.e., companies raise substantial capital through the stock market not banks). The type of capitalism also affects the structure of BOD; in these countries, companies mainly rely on a single-tiered BOD that is usually composed of nonexecutive directors appointed by the shareholders. The main difference between the UK and the United States in terms of directors' roles is that in the United States, the CEO is also usually the chairman of the company but in the UK, the two roles are frequently distinct. Furthermore, in this model, there is a clear separation of ownership (the dispersed shareholders) and directors (who directly manage the company). This separation may generate agency costs[11] due to directors who do not act in the best interests of shareholders but in own self-interest.

Alternatively, the Continental European and Japanese models (existing mainly in Europe and Japan) usually recognize the role of managers, customers, suppliers, workers, and the community in general,[12] that is, the company's duty is to create value for all stakeholders not only in maximizing shareholders' stocks (so-called stakeholder's model or "stakeholder's view"[13]). These two models are also called "coordinated or multistakeholder's models." In these models, companies are usually characterized by a high concentration of capital, and shareholders usually participate in their management and control.[14] In this context, agency costs arise between majority shareholders (usually a family) and minority shareholders. This type of capitalism also affects the board structure with a predominance of two-tiered boards of directors, particularly in Germany and the Netherlands. In a two-tiered board, the executive board is usually composed of executive directors appointed from the supervisory board, while the latter is composed of nonexecutive directors who represent employees and shareholders. Moreover, in this form of capitalism, banks are usually more important than in Anglo-American capitalism because companies raise substantial capital through banks (orientation toward the banking market). This means that banks are usually more regulated and monitored by the national authorities. The Japanese model usually recognizes the interest of banks (lenders) as pivotal; in this context, many times banks have direct participations in companies and control directly management strategies.

Table 1.6 reports how the different forms of capitalism affect CG constructs.

For all of these reasons, CG codes are different across the world and are only applied at a national level. In fact, it would be impossible to create a unique code that considers all of these differences.

It is important to highlight that good CG remain the same regardless of all of these elements, but the means to accomplish this good governance differ substantially based on the factors cited above.

In Table 1.7, we collect the main aspects that characterize the different CG models.

---

[11] In the next chapter, the meaning of "agency costs" will be clarified.

[12] These subjects are called stakeholders.

[13] In Chap. 2, the "stakeholders' theory" will be scrutinized.

[14] The Japanese model is many times characterized by the presence of the so-called keiretsu, that is, companies linked together by cross-shareholdings.

**Table 1.6** How capitalism affects CG constructs in bank and nonbank companies

| CG | CG in corporations | CG in banking | Potential solutions and/or next step |
|---|---|---|---|
| CG models **differ according to the diverse forms of capitalism that are embraced** | Very important problem | Very important problem | (a) Always investigate the different forms of capitalism<br>(b) When regulators decide to issue new CG laws and codes, they should consider what form of capitalism they represent |

Source: Authors constructed

In Table 1.8, the four main aspects to consider when CG topics are discussed are reported.

## 1.2 CG Definitions and the Banking Environment

CG is not easy to define and a univocal definition does not exist. Why?

As mentioned in previous paragraphs, CG is affected by many different aspects (types of capitalism, ownership structure, social elements, legal and regulatory environment, etc.); therefore, these aspects affect the experts' perceptions about the construct of CG, which automatically affects their definitions.

Nevertheless, we have collected some of the most important, interesting, and different definitions of CG that were found during our studies. For each definition, we will try to highlight the following implicit different perspectives.

* The **Cadbury Report** (1992) defined CG as: . . . "the system by which companies are directed and controlled."

**Implicit perspective:** CG is implicitly considered as system that provides direction and control within a company. We have to underline that the Cadbury Report's definition has proven to be very influential in the development of several CG codes worldwide. In fact, many subsequent CG codes have adopted very similar definitions.

* **Demb and Neubayer** (1992),[15] who are two prominent academics, defined CG as: "the process by which corporations are made responsive to the rights and wishes of stakeholders."

**Implicit perspective:** This definition seems to refer directly to the stakeholder's view.

* **Blair** (1995), economist and university professor, described CG as: "the whole set of legal, cultural and institutional arrangements that determine what publicly traded corporations can do, who controls them, how that control is exercised and how the risks and returns from the activities they undertake are allocated."

[15] This definition was quoted in Cadbury (2002), p.1.

**Table 1.7** Different CG models and their characteristics

| | Anglo-American model | Continental European model (also called German model) | Japanese model |
|---|---|---|---|
| Vision | Shareholder's model | Stakeholder's model | Stakeholder's model |
| Ownership structure | Dispersed (absence of a dominant shareholder) | Concentrated (presence of a majority shareholder) | Concentrated (presence of a majority shareholder) |
| Main problems (see Chap. 2) | Agency cost—Management does not act in the best interests of shareholders but in own self-interest | Minority shareholders oppressed—Management act in the best interest of the largest shareholders' (block shareholders) and against minority shareholders' interests | Minority shareholders oppressed—Management act in the best interest of the largest shareholders' (block shareholders) and against minority shareholders' interests |
| Financial orientation | Orientation toward financial markets | Orientation toward banking markets | Orientation toward banking markets |
| General company's goal (linked to vision) | Maximize shareholders' wealth (See Nwanji and Howell (2007), Daily et al. (2003), and Shleifer and Vishny (1997)) | Fulfill the different stakeholders' purposes | Fulfill the different stakeholders' purposes (with focus on banks) |
| Countries | The United States, the UK, Canada, Australia, India, and the commonwealth countries | Germany and other European countries | Japan |
| Board structure | One-tiered | Two-tiered, that is, supervisory board and executive board. *Caveat:* in the other European countries coexist many different forms of board structures (see, for example, the research of Hopt and Leyens (2004)) | Usually, single board composed from insiders |
| Board composition | Usually 2:3 nonexecutive directors and 1:3 executive directors. In general, majority of nonexecutive directors | Directors appointed from the different stakeholders (shareholders, employees, banks, government, etc.) | Solely (mainly) insider directors |
| Hostile M&A and takeovers | Common | Rare | Rare |
| Other aspects | | Germany: Importance of employees and labor unions in appointing supervisory board members | Many times, banks hold stakes in corporations and have representatives on the corporations' supervisory board |

Source: Authors constructed

**Table 1.8** Why is CG difficult to evaluate in companies?

| |
|---|
| 1—Corporate governance regulation and guidelines are a "recent" topic |
| 2—Corporate governance looks at directors' attributes and social aspects |
| 3—The type of ownership structure affects governance composition and goals |
| 4—Corporate governance's models differ according to the diverse forms of capitalism that embrace. This affects board: Composition, aims, and structure |

Source: Authors constructed

**Implicit perspective:** The author's perspective is the social role of the company.

* **Shleifer and Vishny** (1997) provided the following definition: "Corporate governance deals with the ways in which suppliers of finance to corporations assure themselves of getting a return on their investment."[16]

**Implicit perspective:** The authors recognize the central role of investors and their expected returns (shareholder's view).

* **Monks and Minow** (2001, **p. 1),** two important CG specialists, described CG as: "the relationship among various participants in determining the direction and performance of corporations."

**Implicit perspective:** CG represents the relation between systems of "stakeholders." We have to highlight that the authors do not use the term "stakeholders," but implicitly they seem to refer at this conceptual framework. In fact, they mention, inter alia, customers, suppliers, employees, and creditors when describing these participants.

**OECD principles of corporate governance** (2015)**:** "Corporate governance involves a set of relationships between a company's management, its board, its shareholders and other stakeholders. Corporate governance also provides the structure through which the objectives of the company are set, and the means of attaining those objectives and monitoring performance are determined."

**Implicit perspective:** The OECD recognizes the role of all stakeholders.

As we can observe, different regulators, academics, and practitioners have provided very different definitions because of the different boundaries and angles recognized in CG. However, having various definitions can make the CG matter even more difficult to clarify. In our opinion, having dissimilar descriptions can be very useful as they help us understand and describe the perspectives that experts and regulators have about CG topics. Obviously, each reader has a different sensibility about the role of companies (shareholder's view vs. stakeholder's view) that influence their definition of CG tasks and goals (e.g., is the role of CG to maximize a firm's profit or fulfill different stakeholders' goals?). For this reason, we want to leave the reader to decide what is the most fitting definition.

Now that these CG definitions have been introduced, it is time to investigate CG definitions in the banking sector, but the question is do we have an ad hoc CG

[16]At page 738, the authors also define CG as "how investors get the managers to give them back their money."

definition in the banking sector? All of the definitions above can be applied in the banking sector, but we have to consider that banks differ from other corporations in the following ways:

(a) *Systemic risk*: A banking failure can impact the global economy, as we saw with the Lehman Brothers' bankruptcy in 2008. For this reason, CG regulation in the banking sector is usually more stringent than that for corporations and is usually applied at the supranational level. A good example of this is in Europe where the largest banks are directly supervised by the European Central Bank's (ECB) harm called "Single Supervisory Mechanism—SSM," while the national competent authorities (NCAs) (e.g., the Bank of Italy, the Deutsche Bundesbank in Germany, the Bank of France, the Bank of Spain, etc.) have limited supervisory power. This is because the failure of a big European bank would represent a risk for the entire European environment. This requires a global and standardized method of supervision, and NCAs would have difficulty to guaranteeing such an approach.
(b) *Banks create money:* Banks are financial institutions that generate money for the economy (Wray 2013). Therefore, monetary authorities are strongly interested in banks' operativity because their output (i.e., money) is for the public good.
(c) *Subject to more stringent regulation:* Banking regulation is more stringent than nonbanking regulation. As discussed above, banks' failure can have a huge impact on the whole economy. This has pushed regulators to create multiple laws to curb potential opportunistic behavior by bank directors, especially after the Great Financial Crisis in 2008.
(d) *Different types of risks and different methodologies to measure them*: Banks deal with multiple risks daily, the most important of which are credit risk, market risk, interest risk in the banking book, liquidity risk, and operational risk. Nowadays, IT risk and CG risk are becoming more relevant. All of these risks are usually managed and covered using ad hoc instruments prescribed in the banking regulation.
(e) *Different stakeholders:* Not only are shareholders and creditors at risk from banks' activities but so are some unique stakeholders in the financial sector, that is, depositors, transaction counterparties, and taxpayers.
(f) *Different financial structures:* Banks leverage more on illiquid resources from account deposits (short-term resources) than equity capital provided by shareholders, which creates an implicit risk. In fact, banks usually keep only a small fraction of deposits as cash while providing long-term lending for investors and citizens (e.g., mortgages, loans, and credits). This maturity temporal mismatch is a fundamental threat for banks. When several clients start making withdrawals from the same bank's branches, there is a risk of a so-called bank run. The bank run happens when bank's clients believe that the bank may cease to operate in the near future and will start to withdraw cash, which, all together, triggers further withdrawals that can stabilize the bank to the point that it effectively runs out of money.

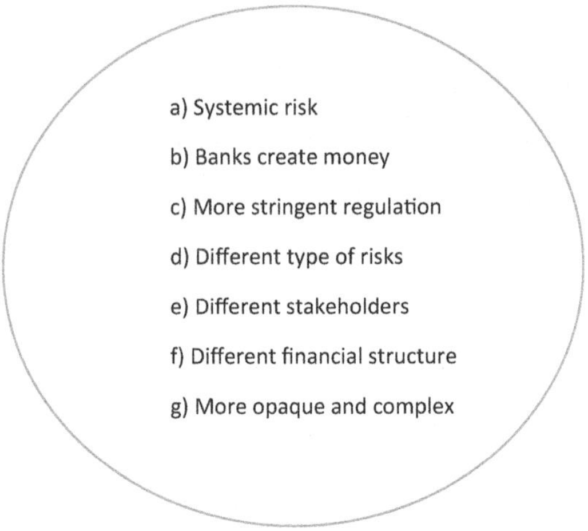


**Fig. 1.1** How do banks differ from other companies (through a CG lens)? Source: Authors constructed

We can affirm that the banks' operativity is based on trust from society and regulatory authorities. Moreover, in terms of financial structure, banks have higher leverage and exposure to capital markets (than nonfinancial firms).

(g) *More opaque and complex than traditional companies:* Banks are more complex than companies. They offer complex products, for example, derivatives, and it is more difficult to monitor bank managers' behavior. This drastically increases agency costs, as we will see in the next chapter.

Obviously, there are plenty of other differences between banks and corporations, but these elements can help us to understand why CG in banks can be different and is regulated differently.

In Fig. 1.1, the main difference between banks is that nonbank companies are described.

An interesting definition of CG in the banking sector comes from the Bank for International Settlements (BIS). In July 2015, the Basel Committee on Banking Supervision (BCBS) published 13 principles of CG for banks that describe the essential role played by the BOD to ensure the decision-making process is correct, thereby guaranteeing a sound risk management system. Through its guidelines, the BCBS defines CG as the following:

> A set of relationships between a company's management, its board, its shareholders and other stakeholders which provides the structure through which the objectives of the company are set, and the means of attaining those objectives and monitoring performance. It helps define the way authority and responsibility are allocated and how corporate decisions are made.

This definition directly refers to the OECD's principles,[17] and the BCBS highlights the crucial role of banks in the global economy that covers some of the areas discussed above.

---

[17] See the glossary of corporate governance-related terms in OECD (experiences from the Regional Corporate Governance Roundtables (2003)).

For example, according to the BCBS, "... Banks perform a crucial role in the economy by intermediating funds from savers and depositors to activities that support enterprise and help drive economic growth."[18]

It describes the different stakeholders in banks and makes the pivotal role of depositors more visible: "... The primary objective of corporate governance should be safeguarding stakeholders' interests in conformity with public interest on a sustainable basis. Among stakeholders, particularly with respect to retail banks, shareholders' interests would be secondary to depositors' interests"[19] (BCBS).

As we can observe, the shareholders' interests are secondary to depositors' interests. This aspect is fundamental as it shows that banks are more than simple companies because they "manage" the money of citizens. CG must consider this point, and for this reason, banks are strictly regulated and supervised. All of these aspects help us to understand why banks need "...an effective board oversight, rigorous risk management, strong internal controls and compliance..."[20] (BCBS). We can observe that BCBS gives a central role to banks' different stakeholders. We will discuss this topic in the next chapter.

## References


Adams B, Ferreira D (2009) Women in the boardroom and their impact on governance and performance. J Financ Econ 94:291–309

Ahern KR, Dittmar AK (2012) The changing of the boards: the impact on firm valuation of mandated female board representation. Q J Econ 127(1):137–197

Anderson R, Reeb D (2003) Founding family ownership and S&P 500. J Financ 58:1301–1328

Anderson RC, Reeb DM, Upadhyay A, Zhao W (2011) The economics of director heterogeneity. Financ Manag 40:5–38

Angbazo L (1997) Commercial Bank net interest margins, default risk, interest-rate risk, and off-balance sheet banking. J Bank Financ 21:55–87. https://doi.org/10.1016/S0378-4266(96)00025-8

Barroso C, Villegas MM, Pérez-Calero L (2011) Board influence on a Firm's internationalization. Corp Gov 19:351–367. https://doi.org/10.1111/j.1467-8683.2011.00859.x

Bartholomeusz S, Tanewski G (2006) The relationship between family firms and corporate governance. J Small Bus Manag 44(2):245–267

Basel Committee on Banking Supervision (BCBS), Bank for International Settlements, Guidelines: Corporate governance principles for banks (Jul. 2015)

Basiruddin R, Ahmed H (2020) Corporate governance and Shariah non-compliant risk in Islamic banks: evidence from Southeast Asia. Corp Gov 20(2):240–262. https://doi.org/10.1108/CG-05-2019-0138

Belkhir M (2009) Board structure, ownership structure and firm performance: evidence from banking. Applied Financial Economics, Taylor & Francis Journals 19(19):1581–1593

Bernile G, Bhagwat V, Yonker S (2018) Board diversity, firm risk and corporate policies. J Financ Econ 127(3):588–612


[18] BCBS Introduction paragraph 1

[19] BCBS Introduction paragraph 2 (2015)

[20] BCBS Introduction paragraph 6 (2015)

Berrone P, Cruz C, Gomez-Mejia LR (2012) Socioemotional wealth in family firms: theoretical dimensions, assessment approaches, and agenda for future research. Fam Bus Rev 25(3): 258–279

Bezemer P-J, Nicholson G, Pugliese A (2014) Inside the boardroom: exploring board member interactions. Qual Res Account Manag 11(3):238–259. https://doi.org/10.1108/QRAM-02-2013-0005

Bhagat S, Bolton B (2008) Corporate governance and firm performance. J Corp Finan 14(3): 257–273

Birindelli G, Dell'Atti S, Iannuzzi AP, Savioli M (2018) Composition and activity of the board of directors: impact on ESG performance in the banking system. Sustainability 10(12):4699

Blair M (1995) Rethinking assumptions behind corporate governance. Challenge 38(6):12–17. Retrieved July 10, 2021, from http://www.jstor.org/stable/40721647

Brick IE, Palmon O, Wald JK (2006) CEO compensation, director compensation, and firm performance: evidence of cronyism? J Corp Finan 12(3):403–423

Brickley JA, James CM (1987) The takeover market, corporate board composition, and ownership structure: the case of banking. J Law Econ 30(1):161–180

Buchetti B (2021) Corporate governance and firm value in Italy—how directors and board members matter. Springer International Publishing. Contributions to Finance and Accounting. https://doi.org/10.1007/978-3-030-56239-7

Byrd J, Cooperman ES, Wolfe GA (2010) Director tenure and the compensation of bank CEOs. Managerial Finance, Emerald Group Publishing 36(2):86–102

Cadbury A (1992) Report of the committee on the financial aspects of corporate governance. Gee, London. Print

Cadbury A (2002) Corporate governance and chairmanship: a personal view. Oxford University Press, Oxford

Cardillo G, Onali E, Torluccio G (2021) Does gender diversity on banks' boards matter? Evidence from public bailouts. J Corp Finan 71:101560. ISSN 0929-1199. https://doi.org/10.1016/j.jcorpfin.2020.101560

Carter DA, D'Souza F, Simkins BJ, Gary Simpson W (2010) The gender end ethnic diversity of US boards and board committees and firm financial performance. Corp Gov Int Rev 18(5):396–414

Clarke DC (2007) Three concepts of the independent director. Del J Corp Law 32:73

Clifford P, Evans R (1997) Non-executive directors: a question of independence. Corp Gov 5(4): 224–231

Daily CM, Dalton DR, Cannella AA (2003) Corporate governance: decades of dialogue and data. Acad Manag Rev 28(3):371–382

Dalton D, Hitt M, Certo T, Daily C (2007) The fundamental agency problem and its mitigation. Acad Manag Ann 1:1–64

Darmadi S (2010) Board diversity and firm performance: the Indonesian evidence. Corp Ownersh Control J 8(2011):38

De Vita G, Luo Y (2018) When do regulations matter for bank risk-taking? An analysis of the interaction between external regulation and board characteristics. Corp Gov 18(3):440–461. https://doi.org/10.1108/CG-10-2017-0253

Demb A, Neubayer F-F (1992) The corporate board: confronting the paradoxes. Oxford University Press, Oxford

Dong Y, Girardone C, Kuo JM (2017) Governance, efficiency and risk taking in Chinese banking. Br Account Rev 49(2):211–229. ISSN 0890-8389. https://doi.org/10.1016/j.bar.2016.08.001

Ferreira D (2010) Board diversity. In: Anderson R, Baker HK (eds) Corporate governance: a synthesis of theory, research, and practice. John Wiley and Sons, New York, pp 225–242

Gómez-Mejía LR, Haynes KT, Núñez-Nickel M, Jacobson KJ, Moyano-Fuentes J (2007) Socioemotional wealth and business risks in family-controlled firms: evidence from Spanish olive oil mills. Adm Sci Q 52(1):106

Gregory-Smith I, Main B, O'Reilly C (2014) Appointments, pay and performance in UK boardrooms by gender. Econ J 124(574):F109–F128

Hambrick DC, Werder AV, Zajac EJ (2008) New directions in corporate governance. Res Organ Sci 19(3):381–385
Hopt, Klaus J. and Leyens, Patrick C. Board models in Europe – recent developments of internal corporate governance structures in Germany, the United Kingdom, France, and Italy, European Company and Financial Law Review. 1, 2, 2004, pp. 135-168. doi:https://doi.org/10.1515/ecfr.2004.1.2.135
Jamali D, Safieddine AM, Rabbath M (2008) Corporate governance and corporate social responsibility synergies and interrelationships. Corp Gov 16(5):443–459
Jizi M, Salama A, Dixon R, Stratling R (2014) Corporate governance and corporate social responsibility disclosure: evidence from the US banking sector. J Bus Ethics 125(4):601–615
Jo H, Harjoto MA (2011) Corporate governance and firm value: the impact of corporate social responsibility. J Bus Ethics 103(3):351–383
Kim KA, Kitsabunnarat-Chatjuthamard P, Nofsinger JR (2007) Large shareholders, board independence, and minority shareholder rights: evidence from Europe. J Corp Finan 13(5):859–880
Kusi BA, Gyeke-Dako A, Agbloyor EK, Darku AB (2018) Does corporate governance structures promote shareholders or stakeholders value maximization? Evidence from African banks. Corp Gov 18(2):270–288. https://doi.org/10.1108/CG-09-2016-0177
La Porta R, Lopez-de-Silanes F, Shleifer A (1999) Corporate ownership around the world. J Financ 54(2):471–517
Lee J (2006) Family firm performance: further evidence. Fam Bus Rev 19:103–114
Liu Y, Wei Z, Xie F (2014) Do women directors improve firm performance in China? J Corp Finance 28(C):169–184
Lubatkin MH, Schulze WS, Ling Y, Dino R (2005) The effects of parental altruism on the governance of family-managed firms. J Organ Behav 26(3):313–330
Masulis RW, Mobbs S (2014) Independent director incentives: where do talented directors spend their limited time and energy? J Financ Econ 111(2):406–429
Mazzotta R, Ferraro O (2020) Does the gender quota law affect bank performances? Evidence from Italy. Corp Gov 20(6):1135–1158. https://doi.org/10.1108/CG-08-2019-0252
McNulty T, Zattoni A, Douglas T (2013) Developing qualitative governance research. Corp Gov 21:183–198. https://doi.org/10.1111/corg.12006
Miller T (2009) Demographic diversity in the boardroom: mediators of the board diversity-firm performance relationship. J Manag Stud 46(5):755–786
Monks RAG, Minow N (2001) Corporate governance, 2nd edn. Blackwell, Malden, MA
Neifar S, Jarboui A (2018) Corporate governance and operational risk voluntary disclosure: evidence from Islamic banks, vol 46. Research in International Business and Finance, pp 43–54. ISSN 0275-5319. https://doi.org/10.1016/j.ribaf.2017.09.006
Nguyen DD, Hagendorff J, Eshraghi A (2015) Which executive characteristics create value in banking? Evidence from appointment announcements. Corp Gov 23:112–128. https://doi.org/10.1111/corg.12084
Nwanji TI, Howell KE (2007) Shareholdership, Stakeholdership and the modern global business environment: a survey of the literature. J Interdiscip Econ 18(4):347–361. https://doi.org/10.1177/02601079X07001800406
OECD (1999) Principles of corporate governance. https://www.oecd.org/officialdocuments/publicdisplaydocumentpdf/?cote=C/MIN(99)6&docLanguage=En. Last accessed 31.12.2021
OECD. (2003). Experiences from the regional corporate governance roundtables. https://www.oecd.org/corporate/ca/corporategovernanceprinciples/23742340.pdf
OECD (2009) Corporate governance lessons from the financial crisis, Directorate for financial and enterprise affairs—Steering Group on Corporate Governance, 23 February 2009, p.2
OECD (2015) G20/OECD principles of corporate governance. OECD Publishing, Paris. https://doi.org/10.1787/9789264236882-e
Pass C (2004) Corporate governance and the role of non-executive directors in large UK companies: an empirical study. Corporate Governance: The international journal of business in society

Petra ST (2005) Do outside independent directors strengthen corporate boards?. Corporate Governance: The international journal of business in society
Pfeffer J (1972) Size and composition of corporate boards of directors: the organization and its environment. Adm Sci Q:218–228
Proença C, Augusto M, Murteira J (2020) Political connections and banking performance: the moderating effect of gender diversity. Corp Gov 20(6):1001–1028. https://doi.org/10.1108/CG-01-2020-0018
Pugliese A, Bezemer P-J, Zattoni A, Huse M, Van den Bosch FAJ, Volberda HW (2009) Boards of Directors' contribution to strategy: a literature review and research agenda. Corp Gov 17:292–306. https://doi.org/10.1111/j.1467-8683.2009.00740.x
Rossignoli F, Lionzo A, Buchetti B (2021) Beyond corporate governance reporting: the usefulness of information on board member profiles. J Manag Gov 25:27–60
Schulze WS, Lubatkin MH, Dino RN, Buchholtz AK (2001) Agency relationships in family firms: theory and evidence. Organ Sci 12(2):99–116
Shleifer A, Vishny R (1997) A survey of corporate governance. J Financ 52(2):737–783. https://doi.org/10.2307/2329497
Shukeri SN, Shin OW, Shaari MS (2012) Does board of director's characteristics affect firm performance? Evidence from Malaysian public listed companies. Int Bus Res 5:120–127
Smith N, Smith V, Verner M (2006) Do women in top management affect firm performance? A panel study of 2,500 Danish firms. Int J Product Perform Manag 55:569–593
Sur S, Lvina E, Magnan M (2013) Why do boards differ? Because owners do: assessing ownership impact on board composition. Corp Gov 21:373–389
The Corporate Governance Principle for Banks. (2015). Basel committee on banking supervision, Bank for International Settlements, guidelines: corporate governance principles for banks. http://www.bis.org/bcbs/publ/d328.pdf
The UK Corporate Governance Code (2018) Financial Reporting Council. https://www.frc.org.uk/getattachment/88bd8c45-50ea-4841-95b0-d2f4f48069a2/2018-uk-corporate-governance-code-final.pdf. Last accessed: 31.12.2021
Turley S, Zaman M (2004) The corporate governance effects of audit committees. J Manag Gov 8: 305–332
Vafeas N (1999) Board meeting frequency and firm performance. J Financ Econ 53(1):113–142
Vallascas F, Mollah S, Keasey K (2017) Does the impact of board independence on large bank risks change after the global financial crisis? J Corp Finan 44:149–166
Van Essen M, Carney M, Gedajlovic E, Heugens P (2015) How does family control influence firm strategy and performance? A meta-analysis of US publicly-listed firms. Corp Gov Int Rev 23(1): 3–24
Villalonga B, Amit R (2006) How do family ownership, control and management affect firm value? J Financ Econ 80:385–417
Wray LR (2013) What do banks do? What should banks do? A Minskian perspective. Account Econ Law Conviv 3(3):277–311

# Chapter 2
# Corporate Governance (CG) Theories and the Banking Sector

## 2.1 CG Theories

Researchers across the world have investigated CG topics leveraging on multiple theoretical frameworks. The purpose of this section is to describe the different theories embraced in CG studies, underlining their main features and differences.

### *2.1.1 Agency Theory*

Agency theory is one of the most important concepts in CG as it helps to understand and describe directors' behavior; above all, it clarifies why monitoring behavior can be fundamental for a firm's success. Agency theory investigates the issues raised from the separation of ownership and control (Berle and Means 1932). An agency relationship is described as a contract under which a principal (the beneficial owner who delegates authority) engages an agent (a person who manages) to execute some tasks and services on their behalf. Agency theorists portray a company as a nexus of contracts between principals (i.e., owners/shareholders) and agents (i.e., people who manage on behalf of principals, namely, top managers/directors)[1] (Fama and Jensen 1983; Jensen and Meckling 1976).

In the agency theory context, the manager's (agent's) function is to maximize the shareholders' (principals') interests (Jensen and Meckling 1976). Unfortunately, when ownership and control are separated, the interest of agents and principles are not always aligned, and the agents may commit a so-called moral hazard (Jensen and Meckling 1976). This theory assumes that *agents are individualistic and intrinsically motivated by the self-interested pursuit of economic benefit.*

[1] Fama and Jensen (1983) describe the modern corporation as a nexus of unwritten and written contracts.

 
B. Buchetti, A. Santoni, *Corporate Governance in the Banking Sector*, Contributions to Finance and Accounting, https://doi.org/10.1007/978-3-030-97575-3_2

For agency theorists, the primary responsibility of the BOD (board of director) is to monitor (control) and limit managerial opportunism and ensure that the CEO and the other directors carry out their administrative responsibilities and duties in the best interests of the shareholders (Fama and Jensen 1983).

One way to clarify how shareholders' (principal') and managers' (agents') interests can be divergent is to describe their main objectives separately. On the one hand, the main shareholders' interest (principal') is to obtain returns from their investments through profits and dividends. On the other hand, managers (agents) may be interested in other aspects, for example, increase short-term variable compensation, career goals, relationship with other CEOs (chief executive officers), and other elements. When the separation between ownership and control is strong (e.g., in public companies where there is a very fragmented ownership structure[2]), the monitoring power on agents' behaviors is very limited and may generate an agency cost, that is, when the management does not act in the best interests of shareholders (viz., it does not maximize the company's stock value) but acts in self-interest (e.g., increase their short-term compensation).

In this case, shareholders unhappy about directors' behavior may sell their stocks ("exit strategy") Agency theorists identified other two methods to reduce the agency problem.

First, improve the monitoring on directors' behavior. Second, align agents' and principals' risk-taking (e.g., through CEO stock options).

In terms of the first method, literature that has investigated the agency theory problem has suggested two important mechanisms to reduce moral hazard problems, that is, a concentrated ownership structure (Shleifer and Vishny 1997) and adequate number of independent board directors (normally at least one-third of the total). When the ownership structure is concentrated, the risk of agents' opportunistic behavior is mitigated by strict monitoring from the blockholders (controlling shareholders).

In Appendix 2.1, how is possible to reduce agency costs when exist a dispersed ownership structure is reported.

**Appendix 2.1 The Agency Costs where the Ownership Structure Is Dispersed: An Explanation**

Let's imagine a world where shareholders only have a small percentage of ownership structure, for example, no shareholders own more than 1% (public companies in the United States have similar characteristics). In this case, when the BOD is appointed, monitoring the directors' behavior and decision-making is limited. In fact, *no shareholder would have the power to raise their hand in a shareholder's meeting* (caveat: the company general shareholders' meeting is the corporate body responsible for approving the removal and/or

(continued)

[2]For instance, there is no blockholder, so shareholders only hold a small percentage of shares.

**Appendix 2.1** (continued)

appointment of the directors) *to propose a new board composition because they do not own enough shares* (i.e., individually they do not have enough power to replace the directors). This is a huge problem if directors start making decisions for their self-interest. For example, if directors know that they will remain just few years in the company (as is usually the case), they could have the incentive to increase their short-term compensation (focus on short-term firm value) without considering the benefits of a long perspective on value creation for companies, how? An example is selecting projects with positive returns in the short term but negative/or no returns in the long term, decreasing in this way company's value and therefore damaging the dispersed shareholders.

Hence, how do shareholders preserve themselves in this context?

The literature proposes the following four possible systems:

First, **shareholders may simply sell their stocks** ("exit strategy"). Once the value of the stock decreases, a new investor who knows that the company is undervalued due to managers' misbehavior will buy all of the stocks and change the BOD and CEO. This puts pressure on directors' part who will limit opportunistic behaviors. Obviously, this can be done only if the company is listed.

Second, you can **oblige** (which usually is only recommended) **companies to appoint a minimum number of independent directors on the BOD** (the CG auto-discipline codes across the world usually require that at least one-third of the directors sitting on the BOD are independent) (*this improves monitoring*). The underlying idea is that independent directors make fully independent decisions because only in this way they protect their reputation in the market for independent directorship. This incentive should make them more effective at monitoring, limiting, and punishing directors' opportunistic behaviors.

Third, **increasing the presence of blockholders** *improves monitoring*. This can be done either buying stocks (by purchasing a sufficient number of shares to have power at the shareholders' meeting) or through shareholders' agreements between small shareholders (e.g., voting pacts). The "voting pact" enables dispersed shareholders to exert a much higher power than the members of the pact could do individually. For example, if 51 shareholders (which have 1% each one) agree about how to vote, they will have the majority of voting rights during the shareholders' meeting.

Fourth, **remunerating directors and high-level managers with (long-term) stock options** aims to align shareholders' and directors' goals in terms of stock value maximization (i.e., shareholders link directors' remuneration to firm performance).

**As we can see, by selecting an appropriate system of CG, it is possible to reduce agency costs!**

**Table 2.1** The agency costs in companies: dispersed vs. concentrated ownership

| The type of ownership structure | Agency problem | Possible solution |
|---|---|---|
| Dispersed ownership structure (also called vertical governance) | Shareholders vs. managers | (1) Exit strategy: Shareholders can sell their stocks. This reduces stock value and puts pressure on managers who risk being replaced through a hostile takeover.<br>(2) Incentive: Remunerate managers with (long-term) stock options. This with the goal is to align shareholders' and managers' interests (i.e., stocks' value maximization).<br>(3) Control/monitoring: Increase the number of independent directors.<br>(4) Control/monitoring: Increase the blockholders' ownership. |
| Concentrated ownership structure (also called horizontal governance) | Majority shareholders vs. minority shareholders | (1) Control/monitoring: Minorities shareholders have the rights to appoint their representatives on the BOD.<br>(2) Control/monitoring: Increase the number of independent directors. |

Source: Authors constructed

Unfortunately, a concentrated ownership structure (e.g., a family that holds the majority of the stocks) may generate another form of agency cost that arises between controlling (e.g., the family members) and minority shareholders. More specifically, the controlling shareholder can make decisions in self-interest, which damages those in the minority (e.g., family members could pay excessive salaries and bonuses to their own board members instead of investing this money in projects that have a positive net present values—NPV[3]; these decisions are also called "private benefits of control"). This happens because minorities do not have enough power to limit the controlling shareholders' decisions. In this case, the literature proposed some methods to reduce this agency cost, and one of the most important was to oblige the presence of minorities' representatives on the BOD or increase the number of independent directors not linked to the blockholder.

Table 2.1 shows the two types of agency costs.

Agency theory in the banking context is predominant; however, banks differentiate themselves because they have different goals and different stakeholders. This generates new forms of agency costs. First, in addition to conventional agency problems that arise between managers and shareholders, in the banking sector, there is a significant risk of opportunistic behaviors at the expense of costumers, that is, depositors and borrowers. Specifically, depositors are a fundamental

[3]The net present value (NPV) is a financial metric used to calculate the current total value of all future cash flows (and cash outflows) generated by a project.

stakeholder. The goal of banks is not only to maximize shareholders' wealth but also, and probably more importantly as previously observed in the BCBS (Basel Committee on Banking Supervision) principles, to protect the interests of these deposit holders.

*We can say that in banks we have a third category of principals, that is, depositors.*

Moreover, banks are traditionally considered to be opaquer and more complex than traditional companies, which can result in intensified agency problems (Morgan 2002). This complexity is due to many factors and directly affects monitoring. For example, stakeholders can have serious difficulties evaluating the quality of the loans granted by the bank or understanding the financial engineering process of complex financial instruments (e.g., CDO, MBS, ABS, etc.). Hence, complexity exacerbates the governance problem. Moreover, the literature suggests that due to the limited liability and protection from deposit insurance (Merton 1977) and implicit government guarantees (Gandhi and Lustig 2015), bank shareholders and directors are very incentivized to take excessive risks (Thakor 2014; Merton 1977), exacerbating the agency costs.

As we can observe, agency costs in the banking sector can be very high. This helps to understand why agency theory is the primary theoretical framework embraced by researchers when they study the corporate governance in the banking sector (CGBS) topic, as we will see in the next chapter. Now we propose a new approach for describing agency costs in banks.[4]

We recognize the following three different subjects in the banking sector:

1. Depositors who have two main interests: first, make sure that their bank accounts are safe, and second, make sure that the bank operates correctly and efficiently (that the bank increases its value), otherwise the bank will stop paying interests on those deposits.
2. Banks' shareholders have two main goals: first, protect bank deposits, otherwise there is the potential risk of a bank run, and second, maximize the banks value and consequently their expected returns.
3. Banks' directors have three main goals: first, protect depositors' bank accounts (otherwise there is a risk of a bank run), second, maximize the bank's value, and third, increase their wealth and power.

In Table 2.2, the different goals of depositors, shareholders, and directors are showed.

Unfortunately, when these goals are not aligned, agency costs arise.[5] As far as we know, no previous research has identified these different agency costs using the following approach.

---

[4]Researchers around the world use the classic agency theory problems when investigating agency costs in banks, that is, shareholders vs. directors (as reported in Table 2.1).

[5]Here we do not refer to investment banks (IBs), considering that deposits in IBs are less relevant. We instead consider a dispersed ownership structure as it is in the classic agency theory.

**Table 2.2** What are depositors', shareholders', and directors' main goals in a bank?

| Depositors' main goals (relevant stakeholder) | Shareholders' main goals | Directors' main goals |
|---|---|---|
| * To make sure their bank accounts are safe<br>* To make sure the bank operates properly and efficiently without taking extreme risks (bank increases its value) and pays interests on deposits | * To protect bank deposits (otherwise there is a risk of a bank run)<br>* To maximize the bank's value | * To protect bank deposits (otherwise there is a risk of a bank run)<br>* To maximize bank's value<br>* To increase their wealth and power |

Source: Authors constructed

#### 2.1.1.1 The First Agency Cost: Shareholders and Depositors Vs. Directors

The first agency cost arises between depositors (principal) and shareholders (principal) vs. directors (agent).[6]

When directors focus mainly on increasing their power and wealth—at the expense of the bank's value maximization and deposits protection—they may augment the bank's short-term riskiness, with the goal of temporarily increasing the bank's gains and fees and thus pushing up their short-term[7] remuneration.[8] Unfortunately, monitoring by shareholders and depositors is limited because of banks' opaqueness. In fact, dispersed shareholders and depositors have difficulties monitoring the quality of the loans granted by the bank and understanding complex financial instruments offered to clients (e.g., derivatives). Moreover, depositor's insurance and implicit government guarantees decrease the interest of depositors to monitor directors' behaviors, reducing the risk of a bank run and incentivizing opportunistic behaviors from directors.

How can regulators, depositors, and shareholders reduce this agency cost?

First, regulators can do so by requiring bank transparency through mandatory disclosures on a bank's risk appetite. This will reduce the bank's opaqueness, subsequently increasing monitoring by shareholders and depositors.

Second, regulators can do so by through correctly calibrating deposit insurance and government guarantees. The idea is that placing a too high state guarantee on bank deposits[9] (or increasing too much implicit government guarantees) reduces the risk of a bank run, which would obviously reduce monitoring by depositors' incentivizing opportunistic behaviors from directors.

---

[6]This is a multiple principal problem (i.e., two principals and one agent).

[7]Usually, directors remain for a few years in the BOD.

[8]This can be replaced with any decision that increases directors' wealth and power while not maximizing banks' value or increasing depositors' protection.

[9]The level of deposits protection in the European Union (EU) is 100.000 euro and in the United States is 250.000 dollars (Federal Deposit Insurance Corporation).

Third, regulators can do so by requiring a minimum number of independent directors.[10] These directors should be able to reduce opportunistic behaviors from banks' executive directors.

Fourth, regulators can do so by incentivizing shareholders' concentration, that is, in this way by giving them more power to monitor directors.

Fifth, regulators can do so by incentivizing banks to remunerate directors with stock options calibrated to consider depositors' interests as well, for example, stock options that are paid only if profit maximization is reached without increasing risk appetite.

Sixth, depositors can do so withdrawing their deposits (first "exit strategy"). The risk of a bank run reduces opportunistic behaviors from banks' directors.

Seventh, dispersed shareholders can do so by selling their stocks (second "exit strategy"). Once the value of the stock decreases, a new investor who knows that the bank is undervalued due to directors' misbehavior will purchase all of the stocks and substitute the BOD. This puts pressure on banks' directors who will limit opportunistic behaviors.

Table 2.3 describes the first agency cost.

As we can observe, regulators, if correctly endowed with powers, can drastically reduce this agency cost, introducing ad hoc regulation on CGBS.

#### 2.1.1.2 The Second Agency Cost: Depositors vs. Shareholders and Directors

The second agency cost arises between depositors (principal) vs. shareholders (agents) and directors (agents). In this case, shareholders and directors are more interested in maximizing bank value than protecting depositors' bank accounts. Directors and shareholders know that in case of bank failure, either the State will save the bank or will be the depositors (mainly) to lose money, paying the higher costs.

Here we have a double moral hazard.

* Shareholders might increase bank risk appetite ("search for yield") with the goal of augmenting gains and fees, as well as their returns (increasing the bank's value).

* Directors might increase the bank risk appetite ("search for yield") with the goal of augmenting gains and fees and so increasing the banks' value.[11]

---

[10] As we will see in the next chapter, independent directors do not always reduce agency costs.

[11] The idea is that directors do this to increase their remuneration because there is already an alignment between shareholders' and directors' objectives (the classic shareholders' vs. directors' agency cost has been eliminated), how? For example, directors are paid with classic stock options; there is a less dispersed ownership structure; the incentive for an exit strategy from shareholders is high; and there is an adequate number of independent directors (see Appendix 1 to learn how to reduce this agency cost). As we can observe, in this situation, independent directors helping to align shareholders' and directors' objective in terms of maximizing the bank's value could incentivize risk-taking, not reducing it! This can clarify why in classic research on CGBS topics, independent

**Table 2.3** First agency cost (depositors and shareholders vs. directors)

| Principal | Principal | Agent | | | | What does reduce this agency cost? | | |
|---|---|---|---|---|---|---|---|---|
| Depositors' main goals (relevant stakeholder) | Shareholders' main goals | Directors' main goals | Agency cost | Moral hazard | What does exacerbate this agency cost? | Regulators | Depositors | Shareholders |
| * Keeping their bank accounts are safe<br>* Ensuring that the bank operates properly and efficiently without taking extreme risks (the bank increases its value) and pays interests on deposits | * Protecting bank deposits (otherwise there is a risk of a bank run)<br>* Maximizing the bank's value | * Protecting bank deposits (otherwise there is a risk of a bank run)<br>* Maximizing the bank's value<br>*** Increasing their wealth and power** | * Directors are more concerned about increasing their wealth and power than maximizing the bank's value or protecting the depositors' money | * Directors increase the bank's short-term risk appetite with the goal of increasing gains and fees and so their short-term compensation (e.g., they increase bank risk appetite by selecting riskier projects with high returns in the short term but negative/or no return in the long term; this is because directors do not remain for more than few | * Bank opaqueness, that is, shareholders and depositors have difficulties evaluating the bank's inclination to take risks and also directors' behavior. The more the bank executes complex activities and offers complex products, the lower will be the shareholders' and depositors' monitoring power.<br>* Depositor's insurance and implicit | (1) Decreasing bank opaqueness by requiring more mandatory disclosure on the banks' risk appetite (moving from voluntary to mandatory disclosure)<br>(2) Finding the correct mix of state guarantees on citizens' deposits or public guarantees (the risk of a bank run reduces opportunistic behaviors)<br>(3) Incentivizing the appointment of independent directors<br>(4) Incentivizing ownership concentration<br>(5) Incentivizing | (6) First exit strategy: the risk that depositors withdraw their deposits | (7) Second exit strategy: the risk that Shareholders decide to sell their stocks |

| | | | | | | | | |
|---|---|---|---|---|---|---|---|---|
| | | | | years in the bank). | government guarantees reduce the risk of a bank run and hence reduces depositors' monitoring on directors' behaviors. | stock options calibrated for considering also depositors' interests | | |

Source: Authors constructed.

How do they do this?

* Shareholders could increase the level of risk appetite established in the bank's statutory requirements.

* Directors could increase the level of risk appetite set in the bank's strategic business objectives and capital planning.

In fact, the bank's risk appetite is fixed (usually) annually by the BOD according to statutory requirements, capital planning, and strategic business objectives. This change is transmitted internally through the bank risk management systems and procedures.

Bank opaqueness, deposit insurance, and implicit government guarantees reduce monitoring by depositors, exacerbating this agency cost.

How can regulators reduce this agency problem?

First, they can do so by increasing disclosure about the bank's risk appetite (as in the first agency cost).

Second, they can do so by finding the correct mixture of state guarantees on citizens' deposits and other government guarantees (as in the first agency cost).

Third, they can do so by requiring that stock options are calibrated to consider depositors' interests as well (as in the first agency cost).

Fourth, they can do so by giving depositors a representation on the board or in other relevant committees, for example, by requiring the setup of a depositors' representative monitoring committee.

... and how can depositors reduce this agency problem?

Depositors can simply withdraw their deposits (as in the first agency cost). The risk of a bank run reduces opportunistic behaviors from banks' directors and shareholders.

Table 2.4 describes the second agency cost.

The interesting point here is that the mechanisms for reducing the two agency costs are similar. This also means that, in this case, these regulators can drastically reduce agency costs, if correctly enforced.

In the last few years, there has been strong pressure from regulators, practitioners, and public opinion on bank directors to consider long-term stakeholders' interest (Leung et al. 2019) instead of the simple profit maximization, that is, moving from a governance model focusing on shareholders' profits (shareholder's view) to a "quieter" stakeholder-oriented approach. In the banking context, it means that the role of depositors becomes predominant.

But what is this shareholders' and stakeholders' approach in literature?

directors in banks often increase risk-taking instead of reducing it, particularly if they have direct financial expertise and there is a one-tier board (please refer to Chap. 3 for further explanation).

**Table 2.4** Second agency cost (depositors vs. shareholders and directors)

| Principal | Agent | Agent | | | | What does reduce this agency cost? | |
|---|---|---|---|---|---|---|---|
| Depositors' main goals (relevant stakeholder) | Shareholders' main goals | Directors' main goals | Agency cost | Moral hazard | What does exacerbate this agency cost? | Regulators | Depositors |
| * Keeping their bank accounts are safe<br>* Ensuring that the bank operates properly and efficiently without taking extreme risks (the bank increases its value) and pays interests on deposits | * Protecting bank deposits (otherwise there is a risk of a bank run)<br>* **Maximizing the bank's value** | * Protecting bank deposits (otherwise there is a risk of a bank run)<br>* **Maximizing the bank's value**<br>* Increasing their wealth and power | Shareholders and directors are more concerned about maximizing bank's value than to protect depositors' money | * Shareholders may increase the bank's risk appetite with the goal of increasing gains and fees and thus their expected returns<br>* Directors may increase the bank's risk appetite with the goal of increasing gains and fees and hence bank's value | * Bank opaqueness, that is, depositors have difficulties evaluating bank's riskiness. The more the bank has complex activities and offers complex products, the lower the depositors' monitoring requirements will be.<br>* Deposit insurance and implicit government guarantees reduce the risk of a bank run and reduce depositors' monitoring on directors' behaviors. | (1) Decreasing bank opaqueness by requiring more mandatory disclosure on the banks' risk appetite (moving from voluntary to mandatory disclosure)<br>(2) Finding the correct mix of state guarantees on citizens' deposits or public guarantees (the risk of a bank run reduces opportunistic behaviors)<br>(3) Incentivizing stock options calibrated for considering also depositors' interests<br>(4) Appointing depositors' representatives | (5) The risk that depositors withdraw their deposits (exit strategy) |

Source: Authors constructed

### 2.1.2 Shareholder and Stakeholder Theories

In literature, reference is made to two approaches to define a company's objective: shareholder theory (also a contractual approach) (Friedman 1970) and stakeholder theory (Freeman 1984).

In the first approach, the company is considered a "nexus of contracts" (Jensen and Meckling 1976), in which the factor to be maximized is a shareholder's value (i.e., maximizing the value of shares, namely, market capitalization) (Friedman 1970). Therefore, the company exists only for this reason. All other subjects or factors exist (customers, suppliers, employees, customers, suppliers of financial resources, etc.), but they all serve this purpose, and relationships are only governed by a defined contractual link. The company does not work to increase the value of these contracts as their value is already defined. For example, an employee's contract is defined by their salary, and they are not owed anything else.

The second approach overcomes this mechanism and states that the company exists to maximize not only the value of shareholders' wealth but also to distribute value to all of the other stakeholders (Freeman 1984). We can say that this is a more "social view."[12] In a stakeholder's approach, the first step is identifying the specific stakeholders of a company and then investigating how managers treat these different stakeholders. Freeman describes stakeholders as "those groups without whose support the organization would cease to exist." This view of capitalism stresses the relationships between the company and its suppliers, employees, communities, governmental bodies, local ecology, financial institutions, costumers, and all subjects that have a stake in the organization. Hence, in this case, firms operate to create value for all stakeholders not just for shareholders.

Shareholder and stakeholder theories do not investigate the relationships inside the board but *look at the company's long-term goal.*[13] Hence, where is the connection with CG topics? Obviously, the goal of the company is translated into the BOD's behavior.

But how can you affect this model from the outside and in the banking sector?

Before the 2008 Great Financial Crisis, the governance and regulatory framework of banks mainly focused on maximizing shareholder's value. Beltratti and Stulz (2012) revealed that banks with more shareholder-friendly boards were affected worst during the Great Financial Crisis. Leung et al. (2019) found that US banks with directors whose legal responsibilities included considering stakeholders' interests reduced their risk-taking by increasing capital and shifting to safer borrowers. Srivastav and Hagendorff (2016) found that risk-taking was exacerbated when shareholder's view governance existed, and they suggested shifting away from this

[12] The social view is not related to political aspects (e.g., socialism); in fact, both theories embrace capitalism as a theoretical framework. Today, stakeholder's view is mainly reflected in CSR (corporate social responsibility) reports (e.g., the sustainability reports) and ESG (environmental, social, and corporate governance) strategies.

[13] Previous research has not investigated this point.

paradigm to decrease bank risk. Anginer et al. (2018) found that shareholder-friendly CG was associated with higher systemic risk for larger banks and banks operating in nations with large financial nets as they tried to shift risk toward the public finances. This last research seems to suggest that more shareholder-friendly regulations can exacerbate systemic risk.

It is interesting to observe[14] that the BCBS in 2010, the first edition of the BCBS "Principles for Enhancing CG," did not assert that shareholders' interests were secondary to depositors' interests. This important change occurred in 2015 with the new BCBS "Corporate governance principle for banks" that seemed to confirm a clear movement from a shareholders' view approach to a stakeholders' view from the regulators' perspective.

In our opinion, both theories have some weaknesses. If we can easily affirm that banks cannot only consider maximizing shareholders' value because they manage and conserve citizens' money (depositors are a fundamental stakeholder for them), at the same time, we cannot ask banks to operate considering all stakeholders' interests because each stakeholder's relationship should be treated, considered, and monitored constantly, according to the stakeholder's view (the so-called identification process).

This continuous monitoring may increase drastically banks' costs and above all could distract the bank from its activities.

We can say that CGBS regulation is moving toward the stakeholder approach.

### 2.1.3 *Stewardship Theory*

Another important theory in CG is stewardship theory, which discards the basic assumption of the agency theory, that is, that managers act as opportunistic agents motivated only by individual utility maximization. Stewardship theory views human nature as altruistic rather than opportunistic. This theory argues that managers are stewards, so their primary motivations are fundamentally aligned with the goals of their principals (Donaldson 1990). In stark contrast with the agency theorists, it suggests that if managers (stewards) are monitored by principals as if they were opportunistic agents, they will feel discouraged and may reduce their cooperation with principals (Davis et al. 1997). This view suggests that managers will instinctively accomplish their responsibilities to shareholders. In this case, there is no need for control and monitoring, which should be replaced with collaboration and empowerment. While agency theory states that monitoring managers can enhance firm performance by reducing opportunism, stewardship contends that managers can improve firm performance only if properly empowered.

[14] Previous research has not investigated this point.

Both agency theory and stewardship theory have been criticized but for opposite reasons. Agency theory was criticized for assuming ubiquitous opportunism, whereas stewardship theory was criticized for generalizing excessive altruism.

Stewardship theory is by far less utilized in research, and only 8% of the research papers investigated in this book adopt this theory as a theoretical background. We can say that, in general, researchers see directors as potentially opportunistic people rather than altruistic stewards.

### *2.1.4 Resource Dependency Theory (RDT)*

The literature has given three main roles to the BOD.[15] The first is control and monitoring, the second is service, and the third is the provision of resources (Johnson et al. 1996).

The roles have been investigated from theoretical perspectives. As we have observed above, agency theory stresses the role of control and monitoring (Sundaramurthy and Lewis 2003), while stewardship theory emphasizes the service role (Donaldson 1990; Donaldson and Davis 1991, Donaldson & Davis 1994). RDT suggests that the board can provide protection and resources to the firm (Goodstein et al. 1994; Hillman et al. 2000; Pearce II and Zahra 1991; Pfeffer and Salancik 1978). RDT describes a mechanism whereby companies have access to critical resources existent in the environment through the affiliations and characteristics of its board members (i.e., directors' linkages).

The directors' role in the provision of resources comprises providing advice, expertise, and counseling, guaranteeing legitimacy (Westphal and Zajac 1994), improving firm performance through their reputation, and operating as a link between the company and other firms and institutions (e.g., relevant connections with external institutions or facilitating access to capital). All of these aspects have the common goal of providing easier access to resources. These elements form the so-called board capital (Hillman & Dalziel 2003).

In Appendix 2.2, some examples of RDT in CG are reported.

**Appendix 2.2 The RDT in CG: An Explanation**

Let's imagine a company that appoints a new CEO who was previously the CEO of an important (current) supplier of the company and still participates in this company. Now, let's imagine that the contract with this supplier must be renewed. We can hypothesize that the new CEO could get a discount or at least will renew the contract with the same conditions. RD (resource dependence)

(continued)

[15] A significant number of studies believe that the distinction between the roles of the board is not clear (see Hendry and Kiel (2004) and Stiles and Taylor (2001)).

**Appendix 2.2** (continued)
theorists in a CG context would say that the director linkage has provided a new resource for the company. The same applies if a company appoints a director that is also a director in the bank that provides loans to the company, and this helps to reduce the financing costs and so on.

Director linkage is not only related to external companies or institutions but can also be associated with directors' other intangible characteristics (e.g., know-how, level of education, past experiences, etc.). For example, let's imagine a chemical company that produces several polluting wastes during the production process. If the company appoints a director that is famous for efficiently managing waste pollution from chemical production, we can expect an increase in the firm's reputation, legitimacy, and probably an improvement in CSR indicators. When investors see all of these aspects, they could be more prone to invest in the company, which increases its market value and shareholders' profits. Also in this case, RD theorists would say that this director has provided a new resource for the company.

As we will see in the next chapter, this is the most utilized theoretical background after agency theory; the 16% of articles embrace RDT as theoretical framework.

### 2.1.5 *The Resource-Based View (RBV)*

Another theory that stresses the importance of managing different resources is the resource-based view (RBV/RBT) (Wernerfelt 1984). While RDT focuses on resources acquired from the environment, the RBV is concerned with the resources owned by the company. The RBV maintains that if these resources are non-substitutable, valuable, imperfectly imitable, and rare, they become the basis of a sustained competitive advantage (Barney 1991). For RBV theorists, the firm is a bundle of intangible and tangible resources (Penrose 1959; Wernerfelt 1984).

How do CG researchers connect this theory to boards?

Well, the RBV in CG topics is mainly linked to directors' characteristics in terms of knowledge, experience, and abilities. The idea is that only these characteristics are harder to for competitors to imitate (they are intrinsically non-substitutable, valuable, imperfectly imitable, and rare) than other board characteristics, for example, the board size, CEO duality, independent directors' ratio, number of nonexecutives' directors, etc. These latter characteristics are considered very easy to imitate, so under an RBV lens, they cannot be considered as a source of competitive advantage. The RBV stresses the role that directors play in providing unique resources to the firm. For this reason, it is mainly embraced by researchers who investigate the relationship between directors' specific characteristics—in terms of background, level of education, and previous work experience—and a firm's performance. This model is contrast with agency theory, and RBV proponents do not see directors as opportunistic agents who control and monitor but as a resource that can increase a firm's value (Hart 1995).

### 2.1.6 *Upper Echelons Theory (UET)*

The UET is generally studied in CG matters and looks at directors' background and personal traits (e.g., level of education, previous work experience, linkages with other companies, gender, age, etc.) (Hambrick & Mason 1984). This theory affirms that directors' specific characteristics partially predict organizational outcomes. UET theorists connect three elements: individuals (i.e., top management teams (TMT)[16]/ top leaders), their strategic choices, and firm performance. UET is constructed on the idea that the characteristics of these top managers (directors) impact and explain the behavior of a company. An interesting point is that this theory assumes that psychological traits (values, personal cognitions, and perceptions) affect any human choice including directors' choices (Hambrick 2007). In this context, a director's background and personal traits are considered as observable indicators of psychological constructs that shape their personal perceptions of the company and so determine and drive the company's strategic decisions (Carpenter et al. 2004). Hence, directors make decisions regarding the path of the company, and these decisions are affected by the different traits and experiences (background characteristics) that characterize each board member.

## 2.2 Conclusions

Current research on CG topics is dominated by the agency theory (as we will see in the next chapter). However, in the last few years, a multi-theoretical approach has been embraced. The idea that multiple theories may apply to the CG domain is not a negative, and CG experts should leverage this aspect to improve their CG knowledge to provide better CG output (e.g., better regulation and research). The following chapter outlines how CG researchers connect these theories to different CG aspects in the banking environment. A positive aspect is that many of these theories cover the same topic under a different lens, but it is impossible to say which theory fits better with CG topics.

[16]TMT is a formulation of directors and top managers within a firm (Finkelstein and Hambrick 1996).

# References

Anginer D, Demirgüç-Kunt A, Mare DS (2018) Bank capital, institutional environment and systemic stability. J Financ Stab 37:97–106. ISSN 1572-3089. https://doi.org/10.1016/j.jfs.2018.06.001

Barney JB (1991) Firm resources and sustained competitive advantage. J Manag 17(1):99–120

Beltratti A, Stulz RM (2012) The credit crisis around the globe: why did some banks perform better? J Financ Econ 105:1–17

Berle A, Means G (1932) Private property and the modern corporation. Mac-millan, New York

Carpenter MA, Geletkanycz MA, Sanders WG (2004) Upper echelons research revisited: antecedents, elements, and consequences of top management team composition. J Manag 30(6):749–778

Davis JH, Schoorman FD, Donaldson L (1997) Toward a stewardship theory of management. Acad Manag Rev 22:20–47

Donaldson L (1990) The ethereal hand: organizational management theory. Acad Manag Rev 15:369–381

Donaldson L, Davis JH (1991) Stewardship theory or agency theory: CEO governance and shareholder returns. Aust J Manag 16:49–64

Donaldson L, Davis JH (1994) Boards and company performance - research challenges the conventional wisdom. Corp Gov 2:151–160. https://doi.org/10.1111/j.1467-8683.1994.tb00071.x

Fama EF, Jensen MC (1983) Separation of ownership and control. J Law Econ 26:301–326

Finkelstein S, Hambrick D (1996) Strategic leadership: top executives and their effects on organizations. West Publishing Company, Minneapolis and St Paul

Friedman M (1970) The Social Responsibility of Business Is to Increase Its Profits. *New York Times Magazine*, September 13, pp 122–126

Freeman RE (1984) Strategic management: a stakeholder approach. Pitman, Massachusetts

Gandhi P, Lustig H (2015) Size anomalies in U.S. bank stock returns. J Financ 70:733–768

Goodstein J, Gautam K, Boeker W (1994) The effects of board size and diversity on strategic change. Strateg Manag J 15:241–250

Hambrick DC (2007) Upper echelons theory: an update. Acad Manag Rev 32(2):334–343

Hambrick DC, Mason PA (1984) Upper echelons: the organization as a reflection of its top managers. Acad Manag Rev 9(2):193–206. https://doi.org/10.2307/258434

Hart SL (1995) A natural-resource-based view of the firm. Acad Manag Rev 20(4):986–1014. https://doi.org/10.2307/258963

Hendry K, Kiel GC (2004) The role of the board in firm strategy: integrating agency and organizational control perspectives. Corp Gov 12:500–520

Hillman AJ, Cannella AA Jr, Paetzold RL (2000) The resource dependence role of corporate directors: strategic adaptation of board composition in response to environmental change. J Manag Stud 37:235–255

Hillman AJ, Dalziel T (2003) Boards of directors and firm performance: integrating agency and resource dependence perspectives. Acad Manag Rev 28(3):383–396. https://doi.org/10.2307/30040728

Jensen MC, Meckling WH (1976) Theory of the firm: managerial behavior, agency costs and ownership structure. J Financ Econ 3(4):305–360. https://doi.org/10.1016/0304-405X(76)90026-X

Johnson JL, Ellstrand AE, Daily CM (1996) Board of directors: a review and research agenda. J Manag 22:409–438

Leung W, Song W, Chen J (2019) Does bank stakeholder orientation enhance financial stability? J Corp Finan 56:38–63. https://doi.org/10.1016/j.jcorpfin.2019.01.003

Merton RC (1977) An analytic derivation of the cost of deposit insurance and loan guarantees an application of modern option pricing theory. J Bank Financ 1:3–11

Morgan DP (2002) Rating banks: risk and uncertainty in an opaque industry. Am Econ Rev 92(4): 874–888

Pearce JA II, Zahra SA (1991) The relative power of CEOs and boards of directors: associations with corporate performance. Strateg Manage J 2:135–153

Penrose ET (1959) The theory of the growth of the firm. Wiley, New York

Pfeffer J and Salancik GR. The External Control of Organizations: A Resource Dependence Perspective (1978). University of Illinois at Urbana-Champaign's Academy for Entrepreneurial Leadership Historical Research Reference in Entrepreneurship, SSRN: https://ssrn.com/abstract=1496213

Shleifer A, Vishny R (1997) A survey of corporate governance. J Financ 52(2):737–783. https://doi.org/10.2307/2329497

Srivastav A, Hagendorff J (2016) Corporate governance and bank risk-taking. Corp Gov 24:334–345. https://doi.org/10.1111/corg.12133

Stiles P, Taylor B (2001) Boards at work: how directors view their roles and responsibilities. Oxford University Press, Oxford

Sundaramurthy C, Lewis M (2003) Control and collaboration: paradoxes of governance. Acad Manag Rev 28:397–415

Thakor AV (2014) Bank capital and financial stability: an economic tradeoff or a faustian bargain? Annu Rev Financ Econ 6:185–223

Wernerfelt B (1984) The resource-based view of the firm. Strateg Manag J 5(2):171–180

Westphal JD, Zajac EJ (1994) Substance and symbolism in CEO's long-term incentive plans. Adm Sci Q 39:367–390

# Chapter 3
# Corporate Governance in the Banking Sector (CGBS): A Literature Review

## 3.1 CGBS: A Literature Review

This chapter presents an innovative and unique literature review covering all of the CGBS articles published from 2000 to 2020. This literature review aims to the following:

(a) Describe the main CGBS areas examined in the literature.
(b) Identify the main CG theories embraced in the banking environment.
(c) Identify the most relevant results.
(d) Make suggestions to regulators about how to potentially improve regulation.
(e) Suggest new research areas.

### 3.1.1 *Selection of Articles*

With the goal to identify the main research on CGBS, we used the Elsevier's Scopus database;[1] specifically, we searched for articles published in the time frame 2000–2020 featuring the expressions "board and bank," "director and bank," and "governance and bank" in the title and/or keywords and/or abstract. This process resulted in 2708 articles being available.

Subsequently, we decided to examine only articles published in scientific journals belonging to the first quartile of the Scimago ranking system. Exactly, the Scimago Q1 collects the top 25% scientific journals according to the SCImago Journal & Country Ranking (SJR) index.[2] This choice is based on the idea to provide a

[1] Scopus is an Elsevier's abstract and citation database. It collects peer-reviewed articles from all over the world.

[2] The SJR is an index of weighted citations per article over a period of 3 years (please refer to https://www.scimagojr.com/aboutus.php).

 
B. Buchetti, A. Santoni, *Corporate Governance in the Banking Sector*, Contributions to Finance and Accounting, https://doi.org/10.1007/978-3-030-97575-3_3

literature review realized using the most relevant research existing on the market. The total number of available articles is 593. Unfortunately, this number contains also studies that have not the characteristics to be part of this literature review. For this reason, we realized[3] the following selection process:

1. We checked one by one if the selected articles effectively analyzed and discussed the CGBS topic.
2. We eliminated the literature reviews and meta-analysis.
3. We eliminated the conceptual articles.

From the first step, we excluded 480 articles,[4] while with the second and third steps, we excluded, respectively, 2 and 13 articles.

The total number of articles scrutinized is 98. The journals with the highest numbers of articles are the *Corporate Governance* (28 articles), *Journal of Corporate Finance* (8 articles), *Corporate Governance: An International Review* (8 articles), and *Journal of Financial Economics* (5 articles).

In Table 3.1, we can observe the 98 researches on CGBS published in scientific journals belonging to the Q1 Scimago ranking by year.

The most interesting observation from Table 3.1 is the significant increase in articles published after the 2008 financial crisis; the number quintuples in the 5 years after the Lehman Brothers bankruptcy occurred in September 2008 compared to the 5 years before the collapse (i.e., 2002–2008), 27 vs. 5. It is clear that during this period, researchers started to investigate the role of CGBS in the Lehman collapse and related financial crisis. The second thing to observe is that the amount of research on this topic did not stop immediately after the crisis but has grown significantly in the following 10 years. The third thing to observe is that CGBS is a very recent research topic (as said in the first chapter), and if we add the number of articles published during the first 10 years (i.e., period 2000–2010)[5] and compare it with the last 10 years (i.e., 2010–2020), the difference is significant (12 vs. 89).

[3]With the purpose to guarantee high research standards, both authors have performed this process independently. The authors have resolved disagreements around the inclusion/exclusion of four articles.

[4]The Scopus database, based on keywords, can generate multiple not relevant results; this happens when common keywords are investigated (e.g., bank). At the same time, this mechanism avoids losing relevant articles. The inclusion criterion entailed that (a) "boards" and/or "governance" and/or "directors" being clearly identifiable constructs in the article, (b) these constructs were studied in a banking environment, and (c) we also removed research that used the search terms with a completely different meaning.

[5]No articles were published in 2000, 2001, 2003, 2004, 2006, or 2011.

**Table 3.1** CGBS articles published over the period 2000–2020 in Q1 Scimago ranking

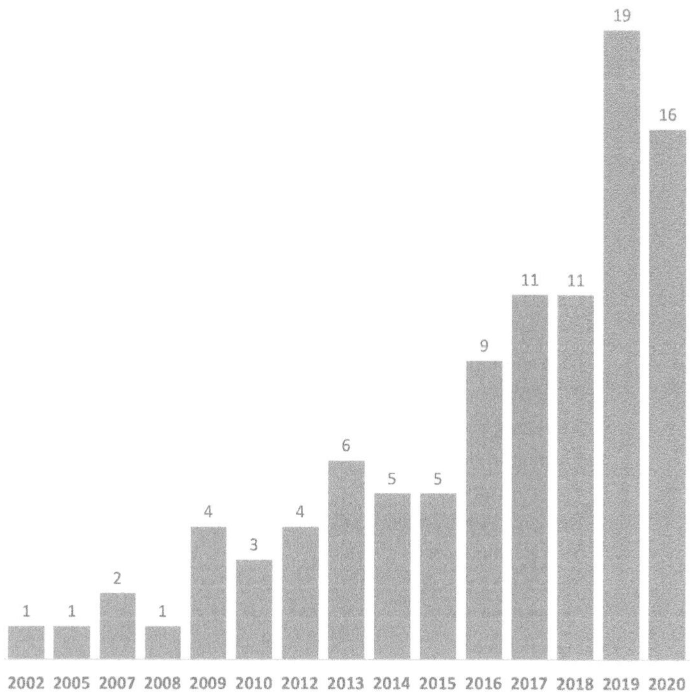


Source: Authors constructed

### 3.1.2 *The Coding Process*

We coded the content of each of the 98 articles.[6] The coding scheme is reported in Table 3.2. For each of the article, we have extracted 8 categories and 39 subcategories. This very meticulous approach is fundamental to perform an innovative and advanced literature review.

[6] Also in this case, both authors have performed the analysis independently. Once completed the coding process, both authors reviewed the classification and resolved eventual disagreements (only 3% articles reported differences in the final output).

**Table 3.2** Coding scheme

| Category | Subcategories |
|---|---|
| 1. Type of article | Quantitative (empirical) |
| | Qualitative (empirical) |
| 2. Main topic | Risk |
| | Board diversity |
| | Ownership structure |
| | CEO |
| | Independent directors |
| | Board size |
| | Compensation |
| | Islamic CG |
| | Committees |
| | CSR and ESG |
| | Political connections |
| | Risk committee |
| | Meeting frequency |
| 3. Theories | Agency theory |
| | Resource dependency theory |
| | Stewardship theory |
| | Stakeholder theory |
| | Shareholder theory |
| | Upper echelon |
| | Legitimacy theory and other theories |
| 4. Setting | US data |
| | EU data |
| | Asian data |
| | African data |
| | Other continents |
| | Multiple continents |
| 5. Country | Name of the country where data have been collected (if available) |
| 6. Listed or unlisted banks | Yes |
| | No |
| 7. Type of banks | Commercial |
| | Investment banks |
| | Cooperative |
| | Mix |
| 8. Source of data | Interviews |
| | Survey |
| | Archival data |
| | Case study |

Source: Authors constructed

**Table 3.3** The theoretical frameworks in CGBS

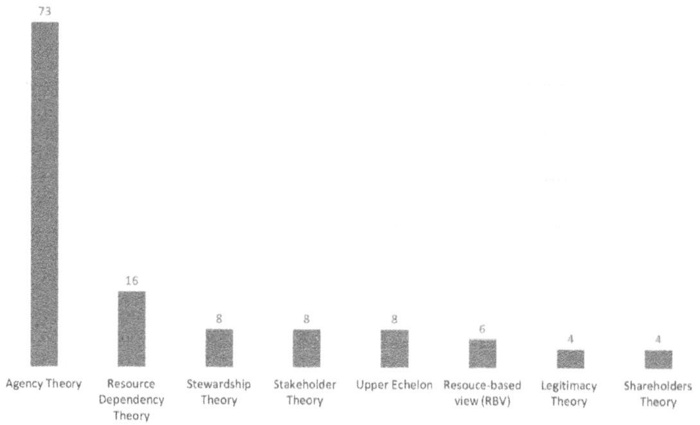


Source: Authors constructed

## *3.1.3 CGBS Articles: Descriptives*

### 3.1.3.1 The CGBS Theoretical Framework

With the goal to investigate what is the most employed theoretical framework in CGBS studies, we have identified for each article the theory (or theories) that the author(s) embrace to shape their hypotheses. Precisely, we have created a variable capturing a paper referred to (1) agency theory, (2) resource dependence theory, (3) stewardship theory, (4) stakeholder theory, (5) upper echelon theory, (6) resource-based view theory, (7) legitimacy theory,[7] (8) shareholders' theory (9), and (10) other theories.[8]

In Table 3.3, it is possible to observe the results; we can see that there exist more theories (113) than the total number of articles (98).[9] It means that on average, more than one theory is employed for each article.

The agency theory is the most relevant theory for investigating CGBS topics with the 75% (i.e., 73) of articles that adopt the agency theory as theoretical framework. Other important theories are the resource dependency theory (RDT) (16%), the stewardship theory (8%), the stakeholder theory (8%), and the upper echelon theory (8%).

[7] The legitimacy theory affirms that a firm can exist only if it acts in congruence with society's values and norms (Dowling and Pfeffer 1975).

[8] The item "Other theories" is not reported in the table.

[9] Five articles did not clearly embrace any theory (or embraced other theories not investigated here).

**Table 3.4** The empirical setting

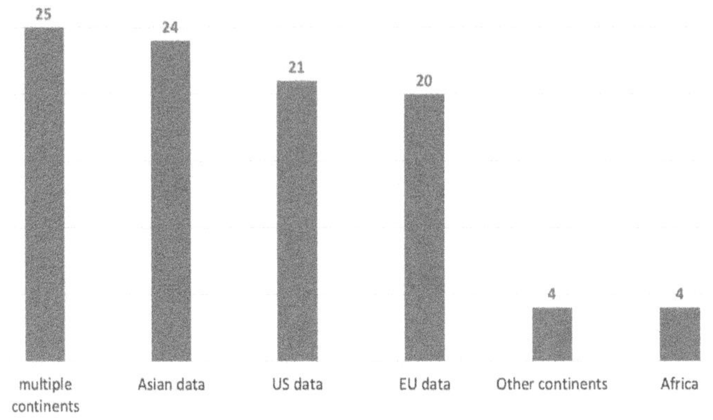


Source: Authors constructed

#### 3.1.3.2 Geographical Distribution

An important dimension of our analysis is to examine the empirical setting in which research on CGBS has been conducted. In Table 3.4, we can observe the geographical distribution of our articles. Six main areas have been identified as follows:

1. Multiple continents: when data derive from countries located in different continents.
2. Asian data: when data originate only from one or more Asian countries.
3. US data: when data derive only from the United Sates.
4. EU data: when data derives only from one or more countries belonging to the European continent.
5. African data: when data derives only from one or more countries belonging to the African continent.
6. Other continents: it covers the areas not included in the previous groups.

The largest number of research leverage on data coming from countries located in different continents is 25 (i.e., 26%). The area with the largest number of research on CGBS topics is Asia with 24 (25%) researches followed by the United States with 21 articles (21%) and Europe with 20 articles (20%). The African continent together with "other continents" has the lowest number of research published in the last 20 years, that is, only four (4%) for both.

The geographical distribution is important because regulation, type of capitalism, and board structure can be very different in each country/continent.

**Table 3.5** Qualitative vs. quantitative methodology in CGBS research

| Type of article | N. | % |
|---|---|---|
| Empirical quantitative | 93 | 95% |
| Empirical qualitative | 4 | 4% |
| Empirical mixed method | 1 | 1% |

Source: Authors constructed

**Table 3.6** Source of data in CGBS research

| Source of data | N. | % |
|---|---|---|
| Archival data | 93 | 94% |
| Case study (s) | 2 | 2% |
| Multiple sources | 2 | 2% |
| Interviews | 1 | 2% |
| Survey | 1 | 2% |

Source: Authors constructed

#### 3.1.3.3 Type of Articles: Qualitative vs. Quantitative

As described in Chap. 1, in academia, there exist two main methods for investigating[10] CG constructs, that is, the quantitative and the qualitative approach. Given the objective to identify what is the most applied methodology in CGBS research, we classify each article in three areas, that is, empirical qualitative, empirical quantitative, and mixed methods. As we can observe in Table 3.5, the empirical quantitative approach is predominant with 93 articles (95%), and the qualitative methodology is embraced only from 4 articles (4%), while only 1 article (1%) leverage on mixed methods.

This is reflected in the methodology utilized for extracting CG data. We classify each article in five categories according to the different sources of data, that is, archival data, case study, interviews, survey, and multiple sources. The vast majority utilizes archival data (92) (i.e., 94%), namely, data that are collected prior to the beginning of the research study. This is the most common data source in quantitative research. It is clear that in the banking sector, the qualitative approach (which mainly leverages on data collected through interviews, surveys, and case studies) is very small (Table 3.6).

#### 3.1.3.4 Type of Banks Investigated

Table 3.7 reports the type of banks investigated (i.e., commercial banks, cooperatives, investment banks, or mixed). Unfortunately, 46 (47%) articles do not disclose this information. More interesting to point out is that 35 articles (36%) examine commercial banks.

[10]Caveat: we do not consider conceptual articles because they are excluded from this research. The total number of conceptual articles was 13.

**Table 3.7** Type of banks investigated in CGBS research

| Type of banks | N. | % |
|---|---|---|
| Not disclosed | 46 | 47% |
| Commercial banks | 35 | 36% |
| Mixed | 15 | 15% |
| Cooperatives | 1 | 1% |
| Investment banks | 1 | 1% |

Source: Authors constructed

**Table 3.8** Type of banks investigated in CGBS research: listed vs. unlisted

| Listed vs. unlisted | N. | % |
|---|---|---|
| Listed | 45 | 46% |
| Not disclosed | 35 | 36% |
| Mixed | 15 | 15% |
| Unlisted | 3 | 3% |

Table 3.8 reports if these banks are listed or unlisted. The majority of CGBS studies investigate 45 listed banks (46%). Only, three articles study unlisted banks (3%). Obviously, the amount of information disclosed from unlisted banks regarding the BOD (board of director) is by far lower than for listed banks. Unfortunately, 35 (36%) articles do not disclose this information.

### *3.1.4 CGBS Articles: Main Areas Investigated*

The articles were differentiated according to the main topic investigated. Precisely, after having scrutinized all the 98 articles, we have identified the following CG areas: risk management and bank's risk-taking (risk appetite), board diversity, ownership structure, CEO characteristics (e.g., education, experience, power and so on) compensation, independent directors, board size, Islamic banking system, committees, CSR and ESG, political connections, risk committee, and frequency of meetings.

Each article has been classified in one or more of these areas. For example, an article that analyzed the relation between CEO compensation and risk management has been classified in three different areas, that is, (1) CEO, (2) compensation, and (3) risk management.

I prefer this granular approach because it gives the opportunity to really deep dive in each CGBS article.

In Table 3.9, it is possible to observe graphically the different CG areas. The most examined topics look at risk management and risk appetite with 41 (42%),[11] board diversity (39%), and ownership structure (32%) research.

In this chapter, we will focus the analysis on the first three areas, that is, risk, board diversity, and ownership structure.

[11] Number of articles that study the topic divided total number of articles (98).

**Table 3.9** Main CG topics investigated in the banking sector

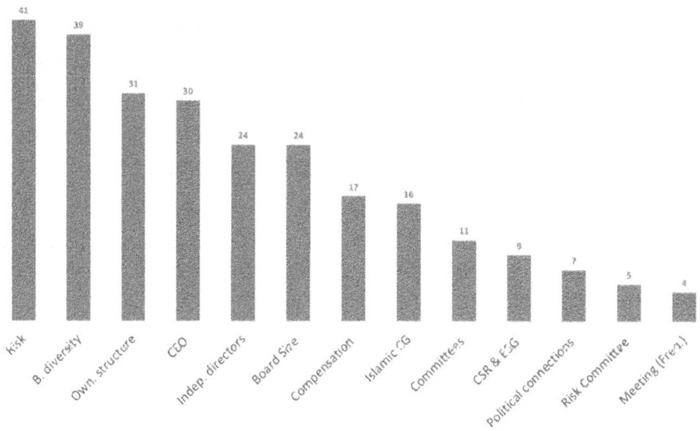


Source: Authors constructed

Considering that each article can be classified in more than 1 area, we have a total of 258 areas on 98 articles. It means that on average, each article can be classified in almost three of the below examined areas.

In the following paragraphs, the areas risk, board diversity, and ownership structure will be explored singularly.

#### 3.1.4.1 Risk

In our sample, CG researchers have tried to find a relation between risk and multiple CG dimensions. Precisely, we have identified these 6 areas: ownership structure (13 articles) (this will be treated in Sect. 3.1.4.3), board diversity in terms of gender (8 articles) (these will be treated in Sect. 3.1.4.2), the proportion of independent directors (8 articles), CEO duality (4 articles), risk committee (4 articles), and board size (3 articles).

##### Risk and Independent Directors

The Basel Committee on Banking Supervision (2015)—in its "Corporate governance principles for banks" guidelines—describes an independent director as

> *... a non-executive member of the board who does not have any management responsibilities within the bank and is not under any other undue influence, internal or external, political or ownership, that would impede the board member's exercise of objective judgment.*

Usually, the banks' BOD assesses the independence of its nonexecutive directors at least yearly.

Several theories suggest that increasing the number of independent directors[12] sitting on the board is beneficial to its effectiveness (Fama and Jensen 1983). The underlying idea is that independent directors make fully independent decisions because they want to protect their reputation in the market for independent directorship (Fama and Jensen 1983; Ferris et al. 2003). This incentive should make them more effective at monitoring, limiting, and punishing directors' opportunistic behaviors (according to agency theory), reducing agency costs, and safeguarding either shareholders' interests (when a dispersed ownership structure exists) or minority shareholders' interests (when a concentrated ownership structure exists). The Appendix 3 describe the importance of these directors.

**Appendix 3 Independent Directors: An Explanation**

Let's imagine that a public company, gyros plc, must decide whether or not to acquire a small listed company, Perlis plc.

Gyros Plc's main shareholder is the Cloe family who hold 49% of the company (the other 51% is dispersed between 51 shareholders that each hold 1%). The family has appointed the CEO and five directors, while six of the board directors are independent. In fact, the CG discipline code where gyros plc is listed states that *when the ownership structure is concentrated, half of the board members must be independent.* The total board size is 12.

In this case, we have a concentrated ownership structure, and the agency cost arises between the main shareholder (Cloe family) and the minorities (the other 51 shareholders).

The Cloe family also holds 100% of Perlis plc stock. Perlis plc is nearly bankrupt, and the Cloe family wants gyros ltd. to save the company by buying it. The only way for the Cloe family to close this deal is to reach a consensus (majority) in the BOD meeting.

Unfortunately for the family, the six independent directors know that this is not good for the other gyros' shareholders, so they vote against the deal because, otherwise, they will never be appointed to other boards as independent directors as they will have lost their credibility as independent members.

As we can observe, independent directors act as advisors, but above all, they monitor the main shareholders' behavior to reduce agency costs.

**As we can see by regulating CG correctly, it is possible to reduce agency costs!**

**Unfortunately, in banks, their role is by far less clear.**

[12]Caveat: the meaning of "independent directors" differs widely between countries (Zattoni and Cuomo 2010).

For all these reasons, the articles below usually embrace agency theory as a theoretical framework and hypothesize a positive relationship between the proportion of independent board directors and multiple banks' risk measures (i.e., an increase in the proportion of independent board directors reduces the bank's risk appetite).

BIS (2006) through the report "Enhancing Corporate Governance for Banking Organizations" emphasized the importance of having independent board directors seating and directly embraced agency theory to describe their significance. The report also suggested that independent directors should have sufficient knowledge and expertise of banking financial activities to "enable effective governance and oversight." The report supported agency theory by explaining the following:

> *....Banks should have an adequate number and appropriate composition of directors who are capable of exercising judgment independent of the views of management, political interests or inappropriate outside interests. In addition,* ***the board of directors has a responsibility to protect the bank from illegal or inappropriate actions or influences of dominant or controlling shareholders that are detrimental to, or not in the best interest of, the bank*** *and its shareholders.* (p. 7, para. 8)

We can see that in the banking sector, regulation and CG theory about the role of independent directors are strictly related.

Here below, the articles that investigate the relation between independent directors and risk are reported. The articles are grouped by setting.

*Asian Data*

Basiruddin and Ahmed (2020) using a sample of 29 full-fledged Islamic banks from Indonesia and Malaysia over the period 2007–2017 find that banks with higher proportion of independent directors have lower Sharia noncompliant risk (SNCR).[13]

Dong et al. (2017) by means of a sample of 153 Chinese commercial banks over the period 2003–2011 show a negative/mixed relation between the proportion of independent directors (i.e., an increase) and banks' risk-taking behavior measured in terms of amount of bad loans recorded in the balance sheet. This negative relation is not statistically significant, but in any case, it goes against the initial hypothesis (i.e., higher independent lower risks).

*Multiple Continents*

Neifar and Jarboui (2018) using a sample of 34 listed Islamic banks from various countries over a period ranging from 2008 to 2014 discover that a higher proportion of independent board members increases the amount of operational risk voluntary disclosure.

[13] Namely, the risk that Islamic finance transactions may be challenged and contested is whether they do not comply with Sharia (Islamic law). For example, an investment in companies that offer goods considered contrary to Islamic principles (e.g., alcohol companies) could be contested.

De Vita and Luo (2018) by means of a sample of 493 banks from 53 countries (period 2001–2015) find that banks with greater proportion of independent directors register higher levels of risk-taking.

Vallascas et al. (2017) utilizing a sample of 262 listed banks (period 2004–2014) from multiple countries find that in post-2009, an increase in independent directors sitting on the board leads to more prudent bank's risk-taking compared to the rest of the sample period. This result is not confirmed for all large banks and most large international banks. Moreover, the authors find that prior to the Great Financial Crisis, independent directors did not help to mitigate bank's risk-taking as expected from the agency theory.

*European Data*

Lu Boateng et al. (2018) exploiting a sample of 79 UK banks (period 2000–2014) find a positive (i.e., in increase in risk-taking) and significant relation between the percentage of independent directors sitting on the board and banks' credit risk level in a one-tier system of boards. The authors suggest that in two-tier board systems, the relation may be the opposite; unfortunately, they do not investigate this point in their research.

Ben Bouheni et al. (2018) examine the relation between the proportion of independent directors and bank's risk-taking using a sample of three French banks (BNP Paribas, Crédit Agricole, and Société Générale) over the period 2005–2011. The authors find that an increase in the number of independent directors might explain the excess in risk-taking of these banks.

*US Data*

Minton et al. (2014) exploiting a sample of 1106 US commercial banks (period 2003–2008) find that independent directors with financial expertise increased banks' risk-taking prior to the crisis (using both balance sheet-based and market-based risk measures).

In Table 3.10, the articles that scrutinize the relation between independent directors and risk management or risk appetite are reported.

It must be noted that an increase in the number of independent board directors not automatically reduces banks' risk-taking but can actually increase it (De Vita and Luo 2018; Ben Bouheni et al. 2018; Minton et al. 2014). If we can detect a reduction in risk-taking for small banks (Vallascas et al. 2017), in large and international banks (Vallascas et al. 2017) particularly when directors have financial expertise (Minton et al. 2014) and banks have a one-tier board (Lu Boateng et al. 2018), we can observe an increase in the banks' risk-taking behaviors. In our opinion, this issue of a one-tier vs. a two-tier board is really important and must be clarified because it can help to explain negative or mixed results.

**Table 3.10** Independent directors and risk in banks

| n. | Year | Authors | Journal | Geographic area | Specific country | Sample | Listed/ unlisted | Type of banks | Period | | Risk management/ risk-taking | Independent directors |
|---|---|---|---|---|---|---|---|---|---|---|---|---|
| 1 | 2020 | Basiruddin R., Ahmed H. | *Corporate Governance (Bingley)* | Asian data | | 29 | Mix | N/A | 2007 | 2017 | Shariah noncompliant risk (SNCR) | Positive |
| 2 | 2017 | Dong Y., Girardone C., Kuo J.-M. | *British Accounting Review* | Asian data | China | 153 | Mix | Comm | 2003 | 2011 | Proportion of bad loans | Negative/ mixed |
| 3 | 2018 | Neifar S., Jarboui A. | *Research in International Business and Finance* | Multiple continents | | 34 | Listed | N/A | 2008 | 2014 | Operational risk disclosure | Positive (on voluntary disclosure quality) |
| 4 | 2018 | De Vita G., Luo Y. | *Corporate Governance (Bingley)* | Multiple continents | | 493 | N/A | Comm | 2001 | 2015 | Measured by insolvency risk, credit risk, and volatility of equity returns | Negative |

(continued)

**Table 3.10** (continued)

| n. | Year | Authors | Journal | Geographic area | Specific country | Sample | Listed/ unlisted | Type of banks | Period | | Risk management/ risk-taking | Independent directors |
|---|---|---|---|---|---|---|---|---|---|---|---|---|
| 5 | 2017 | Vallascas F., Mollah S., Keasey K. | *Journal of Corporate Finance* | Multiple continents | | 262 | Listed | Comm | 2004 | 2014 | Bank portfolio risk | Mixed/negative on large and international banks |
| 6 | 2018 | Lu J., Boateng A. | *Review of Quantitative Finance and Accounting* | EU data | UK | 79 | N/A | N/A | 2000 | 2014 | Credit risk | Negative |
| 7 | 2018 | Ben Bouheni F., Idi Cheffou A., Jawadi F. | *Research in International Business and Finance* | EU data | France | 3 | Listed | Mix | 2005 | 2011 | N/A | Negative |
| 8 | 2014 | Minton B.A., Taillard J.P., Williamson R. | *Journal of Financial and Quantitative Analysis* | US data | | 1106 | N/A | Comm | 2003 | 2008 | Balance sheet-based and market-based risk measure | Negative |

Source: Authors constructed

On a one-tier board,[14] directors who manage the bank (executive directors, including the CEO) and nonexecutive directors (i.e., including independent directors)[15] sit on the same board (i.e., the executive board), but they are two different figures (Adams and Ferreira 2007).

Two elements explain why independent directors can increase risk-taking in this context.

First, outside directors[16] sit next to executive directors, but they have less information and monitoring power over banks' activities (Lu Boateng et al. 2018). Increasing the number of independent directors may exacerbate information asymmetry between executives' directors (mainly the CEO) and independent directors. Independent directors may potentially worsen the quality of the decisions made by executive directors because they do not have access to the same level of information. This also reduces monitoring and allows managers to make strategic decisions that increase the bank's risk-taking appetite with the aim of obtaining the related benefits in terms of future (potential) higher remuneration benefits.

Second, independent board directors (a majority in US context where the dispersed ownership structure is common) are not only responsible for monitoring managers but for providing resources in terms of valuable and distinct perspectives (from the resource dependency theory) (Pfeffer and Salancik 1978; Daily and Dalton 1994; Huse 2005). As nonexecutive directors, they may contribute to control and service tasks with a different level of efficacy (Stiles and Taylor, 2001). In this case, there is a high risk of imparting knowledge and suggestions (from independent directors) that increase a bank's performance leveraging on the bank's risk appetite.

In fact, offering riskier financial products to clients can increase the banks' fees but at the same time may increase bank's risk-taking. Independent directors in this case know that in case of failure, the depositors will pay.

Minton et al. (2014) found that where independent directors have financial expertise, the banks have a higher level of risk-taking. The independent directors know that the risk of bank's failure in this case is mainly on banks' depositors and this can incentivize risk-taking (**this is our second agency cost**).

These two points can help us to understand why independent directors can increase a bank's risk-taking appetite instead of decreasing it.

On a two-tier board,[17] the problems outlined above are mitigated and even disappear (caveat: the two-tier board characteristics may vary across countries). In fact, under this model, the interests of shareholders and the supervisory board are aligned as the monitoring level is stronger, and we can expect better control on a

[14]Typical under "CG Anglo-Saxon model".

[15]In Anglo-American countries, the board is mainly composed of independent directors who usually have two main responsibilities: (a) aligning shareholders' and managers' incentives and monitoring executive directors' decisions (monitoring role) and (b) giving advice and counsel for strategic decisions (advising role).

[16]Here it is understood as a synonym for independent directors.

[17]Typical under "CG Continental European Model".

**Table 3.11** Main findings and suggestions for regulators and researchers (only clear relations are reported)

| Relation | Suggestion for regulators | Theoretical framework | Research |
|---|---|---|---|
| 1.1. Independent directors may increase bank's risk appetite instead of decreasing it. | • Cleary identifying roles and characteristics of each independent director. | • Agency theory. | • Investigating if independent directors decrease banks' risk-taking in two-tier board context. |
| | • In banks with one-tier board, increase monitoring and control independent directors' behaviors. | • Resource dependency theory. | • Increasing multi-continents' research controlling for BOD characteristics (i.e., one-tier vs. two-tier). |

Source: Authors constructed

bank's risk-taking decisions. There are two different boards in a two-tier board: the executive board (where the CEO sits) who runs the bank and makes decisions and the supervisory board whose responsibility is appointing and dismissing executive board members on behalf of shareholders (they also decide directors' compensation and other aspects). In this case, the roles of executives and nonexecutive directors are distinct. Executive directors sit on the executive board, and nonexecutive directors (including independent directors) sit on the supervisory board.[18] Supervisory board members are responsible for guiding and monitoring the executive board.

For these reasons, we can expect a reduction in a banks' risk-taking appetite when there is a higher proportion of independent board directors and the two-tier board system is applied, while there may be a potential increase (or mixed results) when a one-tier system is employed.

In terms of risk disclosure, it seems that independent directors can improve this task.

Table 3.11 reports the main findings and suggestions for regulators and researchers.

### Risk and CEO Duality

In this paragraph, we investigate the relation between CEO duality (i.e., concentration of the chairman's and chief executive officer's responsibilities on the same person) and risk-taking.

Two opposite perspectives help us to connect CEO duality and banks' risk.

First, CEO duality from the agency theory perspective may lead to the failure of an efficient internal control and monitoring system. In fact, CEO duality weakens the

[18] In some countries, for example, Germany, the supervisory board can include employee representatives.

monitoring powers of the boards due to the excessive power given to the CEOs. This power can amplify opportunistic behaviors in pursuing CEOs' personal interests at expenses of shareholders' interests (increase in agency costs) (Jensen 1993; Lasfer 2006; Lewellyn and Muller-Kahle 2012).

Second, from the stewardship theory, the CEO duality is considered as a good aspect. CEO duality can improve firm's stability decreasing information costs and improving firm's performance and organizational efficiency (Anderson and Anthony 1986). We have to remember that under a stewardship theory lens, directors are considered altruistic people who have the only goal to provide resources to the firms with the objective to increase firm's value.

We have to recall that usually CG's auto-discipline codes all over the world recommend that the CEO should not be also the chairman of the company. In this case, the regulation seems to embrace agency theory without considering the stewardship theory.

The following four studies have analyzed this relation:

*European Data*

Harkin et al. (2020) exploiting a sample of 115 UK banks (period 2003–2012) find that the separation of the roles of CEO and chairman (i.e., the opposite of CEO duality) increases bank's risk.

Lu Boateng et al. (2018) utilizing a sample of 79 UK banks (period 2000–2014) find a positive and significant relation between CEO duality and banks' credit risk level, that is, CEO duality increases risk-taking behaviors.

*Multiple Continents*

Neifar and Jarboui (2018) using a sample of 34 listed Islamic banks from different countries over the period 2008–2014 find that a CEO duality decreases the amount of operational risk voluntary disclosure.

*Asian Data*

Dong et al. (2017) by means of a sample of 153 commercial banks located in China over the period 2003–2011 do not find a statistically significant relation between CEO duality and banks' risk appetite.

We can observe mixed results. It is not easy to say which one is prevalent (Table 3.12). Table 3.13 reports the main findings.

### Risk and Risk Committee

Following the 2008 financial crisis, the US government approved the Dodd-Frank Wall Street Reform and Consumer Protection Act of 2010 (so-called Dodd-Franck Act). The Dodd-Franck Act at article 165 required bank holding companies (publicly

**Table 3.12** CEO duality and risk in banks

| n. | Year | Authors | Journal | Geographic area | Specific country | Sample | Listed/ unlisted | Type of banks | Period | | Risk management/ risk-taking | CEO duality |
|---|---|---|---|---|---|---|---|---|---|---|---|---|
| 1 | 2020 | Harkin S.M., Mare D.S., Crook J.N. | *Research in International Business and Finance* | EU data | UK | 115 | Mix | Mix | 2003 | 2012 | Loan impairments as a ratio of gross loans | Positive |
| 2 | 2018 | Lu J., Boateng A. | *Review of Quantitative Finance and Accounting* | EU data | UK | 79 | N/A | N/A | 2000 | 2014 | Credit risk | Negative |
| 3 | 2018 | Neifar S., Jarboui A. | *Research in International Business and Finance* | Multiple continents | | 34 | Listed | N/A | 2008 | 2014 | Operational risk disclosure | Positive |
| 4 | 2017 | Dong Y., Girardone C., Kuo J.-M. | *British Accounting Review* | Asian data | China | 153 | Mix | Commercial | 2003 | 2011 | Proportion of bad loans | No association |

Source: Authors constructed

**Table 3.13** Main findings and suggestions for regulators and researchers (only clear relations are reported)

| Relation | Theoretical framework | Research agenda |
|---|---|---|
| CEO duality is not always negative | • Agency theory. | • Increase research on this topic. |
| | • Stewardship theory. | |

Source: Authors constructed

traded and with total assets above 10 billion dollars) to set up a standalone, board-level risk committee separate from the audit committee.

In Europe, the Directive 2013/36/EU (CRD—Capital Requirements Directives) at article 76 requires significant institutions to establish a risk committee, while Section 5 of the Guidelines on Internal Governance (EBA/GL/2017/11)[19] explains that "...other institutions may also form such committee but are not obliged."

The role of the risk committee should be very important but unfortunately is a very recent topic. For this reason, we have only three researches that investigate its role in reducing bank's risk appetite. Two articles from Asian countries and one from the United States (that leverage on the Dodd-Frank Act reform).

About this topic, the FSB (financial stability board) identified the lack of time dedicated by directors to risk management aspect as one of the main drivers of banks' excessive risk appetite recorded before the 2008 financial crisis. The general idea is that allocating risk management tasks to a separate committee (the risk committee) can reduce risk-taking behaviors increasing monitoring (agency theory framework). Also, in this case, regulators embrace agency theory when requiring the presence of the risk committee.

*Multiple Continents*

*US Data*

Iselin (2020) using a sample of 69 US listed banks over a period ranging from 2004 to 2010 find that banks with a risk committee in place had lower capital ratios before the crisis relative to the banks without a risk committee but higher capital ratios during the 2008 financial crisis.

*Asian Data*

Aljughaiman and Salama (2019) find that the risk committee reduce banks' risk appetite within conventional banks but do not influence the risk-taking behavior of Islamic banks.

[19] Please refer to https://www.eba.europa.eu/sites/default/documents/files/documents/10180/1972987/eb859955-614a-4afb-bdcd-aaa664994889/Final%20Guidelines%20on%20Internal%20Governance%20%28EBA-GL-2017-11%29.pdf?retry=1 and https://www.eba.europa.eu/single-rule-book-qa/-/qna/view/publicId/2013_228.

Yeh (2017) by means of a sample of 78 listed Japanese banks over the period 2007–2008 shows that risk committees can control and monitor efficiently the banks' default risk during the crisis period, but its positive effect is not always statistically significant.

As observed, the number of research investigating the risk committee role in curbing banks' risk appetite is very limited, and the results are many times in contrast (Table 3.14). In this case, new high-quality research becomes fundamental.

## Risk and Board Size

The relation between board dimension and board monitoring has been studied extensively in literature. Unfortunately, the results have been many times mixed, and it is not possible to say a priori if an increase or a decrease in board size affects positively or negatively performance or as in this case the risk appetite.

These mixed results can be explained from theory. In fact, there exist two main contrasting hypotheses existing in literature regarding board size.

The first one suggests that larger boards are less effective at their monitoring role because they decrease directors' communication and increase coordination problems resulting delays in decision-making, that is, increase agency costs (Hermalin and Weisbach 2003; Dong et al. 2017).

The second one at the opposite says that monitoring increases with board size because it increases the number of directors with different expertise (Andres and Vallelado 2008; Wang and Hsu 2013) (in this case, for example, with risk management expertise).

### *Asian Data*

Basiruddin and Ahmed (2020) using a sample of 29 full-fledged Islamic banks from Indonesia and Malaysia over the period 2007–2017 find that banks with smaller board size have lower Sharia noncompliant risk (SNCR).

### *European Data*

Lu Boateng et al. (2018) by means of a sample of 79 UK banks over the period 2000–2014 find a negative and significant relation between board size and banks' credit risk level (i.e., an increase in board size reduces credit risk level for UK banks).

### *Multiple Continents*

De Vita and Luo (2018) by means of a sample of 493 banks from 53 countries (period 2001–2015) find that banks with greater board size register higher levels of risk-taking.

Unfortunately, also in the banking sector, we have mixed results (Table 3.15).

**Table 3.14** Risk committee and risks in banks

| n. | Year | Authors | Journal | Geographic area | Specific country | Sample | Listed / unlisted | Type of banks | Period | | Risk management/ risk-taking | Risk committee |
|---|---|---|---|---|---|---|---|---|---|---|---|---|
| 1 | 2020 | Iselin M. | *Journal of Accounting and Public Policy* | (1) US data | | 69 | Listed | N/A | 2004 | 2010 | Capital ratios | Positive/ mixed |
| 2 | 2019 | Aljughaiman A.A., Salama A. | *Journal of Accounting and Public Policy* | (5) Multiple continents | Middle East and North Africa (MENA) region | 65 | Listed | Comm | 2005 | 2015 | Risk index | Positive/ mixed |
| 3 | 2017 | Yeh T.-M. | *Corporate Governance (Bingley)* | (3) Asian data | Japan | 78 | Listed | N/A | 2007 | 2008 | Default risk | Positive/ mixed |

Source: Authors constructed

**Table 3.15** Board size and risk in banks

| n. | Year | Authors | Journal | Geographic area | Specific country | Sample | Listed / unlisted | Type of banks | Period | | Risk management/ risk-taking | Board size (larger) |
|---|---|---|---|---|---|---|---|---|---|---|---|---|
| 1 | 2020 | Basiruddin R., Ahmed H. | *Corporate Governance (Bingley)* | Asian data | | 29 | Mix | N/A | 2007 | 2017 | Shariah noncompliant risk (SNCR) | Negative |
| 2 | 2018 | De Vita G., Luo Y. | *Corporate Governance (Bingley)* | Multiple continents | | 493 | N/A | Comm | 2001 | 2015 | Risk index | Negative |
| 3 | 2018 | Lu J., Boateng A. | *Review of Quantitative Finance and Accounting* | EU data | UK | 79 | N/A | N/A | 2000 | 2014 | Credit risk | Positive |

Source: Authors constructed

#### 3.1.4.2 Board Diversity

Board diversity (also called board heterogeneity) is described in literature as a potential mechanism to improve bank governance. The general idea is that diversity (in terms of gender, age, ethnicity, work experience education, etc.) can provide unique sources (from the resource dependency theory) to the board (Johnson et al. 1996) and can generate cognitive conflict between board members generating an enhancement of board of directors' independence of thought and so improving the advising and monitoring functions (from the agency theory) reducing groupthink (Francoeur et al. 2008).

About diversity in Europe is really important to cite the recital 60 of the Directive 2013/36/EU (CRD—Capital Requirements Directives):

*The lack of "monitoring" by management bodies of management decisions is partly due to the phenomenon of "groupthink."*

In this phrase, the regulator indirectly refers to the agency theory.

After it continues:

*This phenomenon is, inter alia, caused by a lack of diversity in the composition of management bodies. To facilitate independent opinions and critical challenge, management bodies of institutions should therefore be sufficiently diverse as regards age, gender, geographical provenance and educational and professional background to present a variety of views and experiences. Gender balance is of particular importance to ensure adequate representation of population. In particular, institutions not meeting a threshold for representation of the underrepresented gender should take appropriate action as a matter of priority…*

*… More diverse management bodies should more effectively monitor management and therefore contribute to improved risk oversight and resilience of institutions.*

*… Therefore, diversity should be one of the criteria for the composition of management bodies. Diversity should also be addressed in institutions' recruitment policy more generally. Such a policy should, for instance, encourage institutions to select candidates from shortlists including both genders.*

The regulator identifies diversity as a tool for increasing monitoring and so reducing banks' risk-taking.

In this part, we focus only on gender diversity. That is by far the most studied aspect when we talk about diversity in CG.

##### Gender Diversity

The most recent CG literature has acknowledged that gender diversity on the board of directors may affect the efficiency and functioning of boards and committees (see, for example, Adams and Ferreira (2012), Erhardt et al. (2003), and Caspar (2007))

In our sample, CG researchers have tried to find a relation between gender diversity and multiple banks' characteristics. Precisely, we have identified these seven areas: performance measures, risk-taking level, earnings and accounting quality, CSR, level of banks' efficiency, compensation, and other residual items.

In the following paragraphs, we analyze how gender impact on these seven areas according to this research.

*Gender Diversity and Performance*

In literature, the relation between gender and firms' performance has been investigated deeply from different authors; unfortunately, the results are strongly in contrast to each other. Some authors find a positive relation (Liu et al. 2014; Lückerath-Rovers 2013; Campbell and Minguez-Vera 2008; Joy et al. 2007) and others a negative link (Ahern and Dittmar 2012; Adams and Ferreira 2009), and some do not find any significant relation (Gregory-Smith et al. 2014; Caspar 2007; Farrell and Hersch 2005).

In our sample, six studies have investigated the relation between gender diversity and performance.

*European Data*

Mazzotta and Ferraro (2020) by means of a sample of 22 listed Italian banks over the period 2008–2011 show a positive relation between performance (accounting measures) and gender diversity and a negative relation with market performance.

Cardillo et al. (2020) using a sample of listed EU banks over the period 2005–2017 find that gender diversity is positively related with performance although gender diverse boards have a lower probability to receive a public bailout.

Proença et al. (2020) using a sample of 83 ECB supervised banks (period 2012–2017) show that when gender diversity is high, there is a U-shaped nonlinear relationship between political connections and banking performance.

We can observe that at European level, the relation between gender diversity and banks' performance is not clearly identifiable.

For Africa, Asia, and the United States, we find one article per each area.

Kusi et al. (2018) exploiting a sample of 267 African banks (period 2006–2011) find no relation between the proportion of women sitting on the board and performance.

Dong et al. (2017) by means of a sample of 153 commercial banks located in China over the period 2003–2011 show that board gender diversity has a positive influence on performance.

Nguyen (2015) using a sample of 308 US listed banks over the period 1999–2011 find that board gender diversity has not been affected on banks' performance.

Also in this case, it is not possible to identify a clear relation between gender diversity and performance, except for China. Unfortunately, only one research investigates this topic.

Globally, if we consider all these six researches, the effect of gender diversity on banks' performance is far from clear. This requires new research.

In Table 3.16, it is possible to observe the six articles above analyzed.

**Table 3.16** Gender diversity and performance in banks

| n. | Year | Authors | Journal | Geographic area | Specific country | Sample | Listed/unlisted | Type of banks | Period | | Gender variables | Performance |
|---|---|---|---|---|---|---|---|---|---|---|---|---|
| 1 | 2020 | Mazzotta R., Ferraro O. | *Corporate Governance* | EU data | Italy | 22 | Listed | N/A | 2008 | 2014 | Prop. female directors | Mixed results |
| 2 | 2020 | Proença C., Augusto M., Murteira J. | *Corporate Governance* | EU data | EU | 83 | Listed | N/A | 2013 | 2017 | Prop. female directors | Mixed results |
| 3 | 2020 | Cardillo G., Onali E., Torluccio G. | *Journal of Corporate Finance* | EU data | EU | 83 | Listed | Mix | 2005 | 2017 | Prop. female directors | Positive |
| 4 | 2018 | Kusi B.A., Gyeke-Dako A., Agbloyor E.K., Darku A.B. | *Corporate Governance* | Africa | | 267 | N/A | Mix | 2006 | 2011 | Prop. female directors | No association |
| 5 | 2017 | Dong Y., Girardone C., Kuo J.-M. | *British Accounting Review* | Asian data | China | 153 | Mix | Commercials | 2003 | 2011 | Prop. female directors | Positive |
| 6 | 2015 | Nguyen D.D.L., Hagendorff J., Eshraghi A. | *Corporate Governance: An International Review* | US data | | 308 | Listed | N/A | 1999 | 2011 | Prop. female directors | No association |

Source: Authors constructed

*Gender Diversity and Risks*

The relation between gender diversity and risk has been investigated in eight articles.

*Multiple Continents*

Birindelli et al. (2020) examine the relation between women directors and bank's risk using a sample of 215 listed banks from 40 countries over the period 2008–2016. The authors find that increasing the number of women directors when banks are unsound does not reduce bank's risk; at the opposite, increasing the number of women directors when banks are sound decreases bank's risk-taking but only if their amount does not reach a critical mass.

De Vita and Luo (2018) by means of a sample of 493 banks from 53 countries (period 2001–2015) find that banks with greater gender diversity register higher levels of risk-taking.

We can observe two opposite results. Also, in this case, the relation between gender and the level of risk-taking is not clearly identifiable.

*US Data*

Palvia et al. (2020) using a sample of US unlisted commercial banks over a period ranging from 2007 to 2012 find that when banks' chairpersons and CEOs are female, the banks have a lower default risk in the aftermath of real estate price shocks.

Palvia et al. (2015) find that banks with female CEOs hold more conservative levels of capital. The authors use a sample of 6729 US commercial banks over the period 2007–2010.

Both studies leverage on very large samples. It looks clear a positive relation between gender diversity and a reduction in bank's risk-taking in the US setting.

*European Data*

Lu and Boateng (2018) by means of a sample of 79 UK banks (period 2000–2014) find a negative relation between the proportion of women sitting on the board and the level of risk-taking measured in terms of credit risk.

Berger et al. (2014) exploiting a sample of 15,414 German banks (period 1994–2010) find no relation between gender diverse board and the level of risk-taking.

De Cabo et al. (2012) using a sample of 612 European banks (period 1998–2004) find that the proportion of women on the board is higher for lower-risk banks.

Also in this case, when we look at European data, the results are at odds.

*Asian Data*

Dong et al. (2017) by means of a sample of 153 commercial banks located in China over the period 2003–2011 show that board gender diversity has a positive influence on the level of traditional bank's risks.

Also, in this case, Dong et al. (2017) find a positive impact from gender diverse board.

Globally, we can say there is no clear evidence that gender diverse boards can affect banks' risk-taking, with the exception of the United States and China where there is evidence that increasing the proportion of women sitting on the board and/or appointing female CEO directors can reduce the level of risk-taking (Table 3.17). This aspect is really interesting, and it should be considered from regulators of these two geographic areas. For European data, it is needed to increase the amount of research on this topic.

*Gender Diversity and CSR*

Regarding the relation between gender diversity and corporate social responsibility, we have four researches: two that cover multiple countries and two in Asian countries. There is no research with only European or US data.

*Multiple Continents*

Tapver et al. (2020) find a positive association between the proportion of female directors and the level of banks' CSR disclosure in a sample of 285 listed banks from multiple countries over the period 2005–2017.

Birindelli et al. (2019) using a sample of 96 listed banks in the EMEA region (period 2011–2016) do not find a linear relation between environmental performance of banks and the proportion of female directors sitting on the board.

These articles find a positive association between the proportion of female directors and the level of banks' CSR disclosure using a sample of banks located in multiple countries. Instead, if we look instead at the relation between gender diversity and environmental performance, we do not observe a clear linear relation.

*Asian Data*

Orazalin (2019) by means of a sample of 38 listed banks in Kazakhstan over the period 2010–2016 shows that board gender diversity has a positive influence on the level of CSR disclosure.

Kiliç (2015) by means of a sample of 25 Turkish banks over the period 2008–2012 finds that board gender diversity has a significant positive effect on CSR disclosure.

Both studies find a positive relation between the proportion of female directors sitting on the board and the level of CSR disclosure.

**Table 3.17** Gender diversity and risk in banks

| n. | Year | Authors | Journal | Geographic area | Specific country | Sample | Listed/ unlisted | Sample period | Year (sample) | | Gender variables | Risk |
|---|---|---|---|---|---|---|---|---|---|---|---|---|
| 1 | 2020 | Birindelli G., Chiappini H., Savioli M. | *Corporate Governance* | Multiple continents | | 215 | Listed | Mix | 2008 | 2016 | Prop. female directors | Positive/ no association |
| 2 | 2018 | De Vita G., Luo Y. | *Corporate Governance* | Multiple continents | | 493 | N/A | Commercials | 2001 | 2015 | Prop. female directors | Negative |
| 3 | 2020 | Palvia A., Vähämaa E., Vähämaa S. | *Journal of Business Research* | US data | | 6971 | Unlisted | Commercials | 2007 | 2017 | Female CEO/chairperson | Positive |
| 4 | 2014 | Palvia A., Vähämaa E., Vähämaa S. | *Journal of Business Ethics* | US data | | 6729 | Mix | Commercials | 2007 | 2010 | Female CEO/chairperson | Positive |
| 5 | 2018 | Lu J., Boateng A. | *Review of Quantitative Finance and Accounting* | EU data | UK | 79 | N/A | N/A | 2000 | 2014 | Prop. female directors | Negative |

| | | | | | | | | | | | | |
|---|---|---|---|---|---|---|---|---|---|---|---|---|
| 6 | 2014 | Berger A. N., Kick T., Schaeck K. | *Journal of Corporate Finance* | EU data | Germany | 15,414 | N/A | N/A | 1994 | 2010 | Female CEO/chairperson | No association |
| 7 | 2012 | de Cabo R. M., Gimeno R., Nieto M.J. | *Journal of Business Ethics* | EU data | | 612 | Mix | Mix | 1998 | 2004 | Prop. female directors | Positive |
| 8 | 2017 | Dong Y., Girardone C., Kuo J.-M. | *British Accounting Review* | Asian data | China | 153 | Mix | Commercials | 2003 | 2011 | Prop. female directors | Positive |

Source: Authors constructed

Globally, we can observe (Table 3.18) a clear positive relation between gender diverse board and the level of corporate disclosure. In this case, it would be interesting to investigate if this relation is present also at European and US level (Table 3.19).

*Gender Diversity and Efficiency*

The relation between gender diverse board and bank's efficiency has been investigated in three researches: one in Africa and two in Asia.

*African Data*

Adeabah et al. (2019) using a sample of 21 African commercial banks during the period 2009–2017 find that gender diversity promotes bank efficiency.

*Asian Data*

Ramly et al. (2017) by means of a sample of 102 commercial banks located in the ASEAN-5 countries over the period 1999–2012 show that female directors on boards are more effective in improving banks' efficiency only if they are also appointed as independent directors.

Dong et al. (2017) by means of a sample of 153 commercial banks located in China over the period 2003–2011 show that board gender diversity has a positive influence on cost-efficiency.

In these three researches, there is a positive relation between bank's efficiency and gender diverse board. Unfortunately, no research with data from multiple continents, Europe, and the United States are available (Table 3.20). Hence, at the moment, we cannot generalize these results.

*Gender Diversity and Compensation, Accounting Quality, and Others*

Regarding the relation between gender diverse board and compensation, only two researches are available: one in Asia and the other one in Spain.

*Asian Data*

Ting and Huang (2018) find a positive association between the proportion of female directors and a reduction in the number of perks (compensation) in a sample of 140 Chinese banks over the period 1999–2011.

*European Data*

García-Meca (2016) exploiting a sample of 44 Spanish savings banks located (period 2004–2009) finds that female directors reduce managers' compensation.

**Table 3.18** Gender diversity and CSR disclosure in banks

| n. | Year | Authors | Journal | Geographic area | Specific country | Sample | Listed/ unlisted | Sample period | Year (sample) | | Gender variables | CSR |
|---|---|---|---|---|---|---|---|---|---|---|---|---|
| 1 | 2020 | Tapver T., Laidroo L., Gurvitš-Suits N.A. | *Corporate Governance* | Multiple continents | | 285 | Listed | Commercials | 2005 | 2017 | Prop. female directors | Positive |
| 2 | 2019 | Birindelli G., Iannuzzi A. P., Savioli M. | *Corporate Social Responsibility and Environmental Management* | Multiple continents | | 96 | Listed | Mix | 2011 | 2016 | Prop. female directors | No association |
| 3 | 2019 | Orazalin N. | *Corporate Governance* | Asian data | Kazakhstan | 38 | Listed | Commercials | 2010 | 2016 | Prop. female directors | Positive |
| 4 | 2015 | Kiliç M., Kuzey C., Uyar A. | *Corporate Governance* | Asian data | Turkey | 25 | N/A | N/A | 2008 | 2012 | Prop. female directors | Positive |

Source: Authors constructed

**Table 3.19** Main findings and suggestions for regulators and researchers (only clear relations are reported)

| Relation | Theoretical framework | Research |
|---|---|---|
| Women directors may improve CSR disclosure | • Agency theory.<br>• Resource dependency theory. | • Investigating whether this relation holds also in Europe, the United States, and Africa. |

Source: Authors constructed

In both researches, it is clear that female directors increase monitoring reducing excessive compensation. No data regarding banks located in multiple countries, the United States, or Africa are available (Table 3.21). This is a real pity because it seems to exist a strong relation between gender diverse boards and mitigation of excessive compensation (Table 3.22).

Only one European research investigates the relation between board gender diversity and accounting quality.

*European Data*

García-Sánchez et al. (2017) exploiting a sample of 159 banks located in 9 different countries (period 2004–2010) finds that female directors positively affect earnings quality and accounting conservatism in banks.

The relation between gender diversity and accounting quality seems to be positive. Unfortunately, in this case, just one research is available on this topic (Table 3.23).

The last research on gender diversity does not cover any of the area abovementioned. This research looks at the relation between CEO power and board diversity in Chinese banks.

*Asian Data*

Ting et al. (2017) using a sample of 140 Chinese banks over the period 1991–2011 find that when the CEOs have "structural power" (i.e., CEO duality), there is an increase in gender board diversity. The authors also find that when CEOs have "expert power" (i.e., CEO's tenure), the banks perform better and have a more gender diversified board (Table 3.24).

#### 3.1.4.3 Ownership Structure

The relation between ownership structures and banks' characteristics has been studied extensively in the last 20 years. In our sample, we have 31 articles (i.e., one-third of the total) that explore this subject. Here below we analyze the main areas investigated:

**Table 3.20** Gender diversity and efficiency in banks

| n. | Year | Authors | Journal | Geographic area | Specific country | Sample | Listed/ unlisted | Sample period | Year (sample) | | Gender variables | Efficiency |
|---|---|---|---|---|---|---|---|---|---|---|---|---|
| 1 | 2019 | Adeabah D., Gyeke-Dako A., Andoh C. | *Corporate Governance* | Africa | | 21 | N/A | Commercials | 2009 | 2017 | Prop. female directors | Positive |
| 2 | 2017 | Ramly Z., Chan S.-G., Mustapha M.Z., Sapiei N.S. | *Review of Managerial Science* | Asian data | | 102 | N/A | Commercials | 1999 | 2012 | Prop. female directors | Positive/ mixed |
| 3 | 2017 | Dong Y., Girardone C., Kuo J.-M. | *British Accounting Review* | Asian data | China | 153 | Mix | Commercials | 2003 | 2011 | Prop. female directors | Positive |

Source: Authors constructed

**Table 3.21** Gender diversity and directors' compensation in banks

| n. | Year | Authors | Journal | Geographic area | Specific country | Sample | Listed/ unlisted | Sample period | Year (sample) | | Gender variables | Compensation |
|---|---|---|---|---|---|---|---|---|---|---|---|---|
| 1 | 2018 | Ting H.-I., Huang P.-K. | *Journal of Economics and Business* | Asian data | China | 140 | N/A | N/A | 1999 | 2011 | Prop. female directors | Positive |
| 2 | 2016 | García-Meca E. | *Review of Managerial Science* | EU data | Spain | 44 | Listed | Commercials | 2004 | 2009 | Prop. female directors | Positive |

Source: Authors constructed

**Table 3.22** Main findings and suggestions for regulators and researchers (only clear relations are reported)

| Relation | Theoretical framework | Research |
|---|---|---|
| 1.2. Women directors may reduce compensation. | • Agency theory.<br>• Resource dependency theory. | • Investigating whether this relation holds also in the United States and Africa. |

Source: Authors constructed

(a) The role of foreign shareholders.
(b) The effect of a concentrated ownership structure.
(c) The state's participation.
(d) Directors' stock ownership.

## Foreign Ownership Structure

The first relation is between foreign ownership and banks' different characteristics. Foreign ownership (or foreign shareholders' presence) is frequently considered as positive aspect; this is because usually foreigner investors introduce the best CG practices (Brewster et al. 2008) and bring risk management system improving performance (Berger et al. 2009).

### *Foreign Ownership Structure and Performance*

The first relation is between foreign ownership and banks' different measures of performance.

#### *Asian Data*

Rashid et al. (2020) find a positive association between foreign ownership structure and total financial productivity in a sample of 30 listed banks from Bangladesh over the period 2003–2017.

Chahal and Kumari (2013) by means of a sample of one bank over the period 1996–2007 show that foreign shareholders (together with shares held by different individuals and legal entities) are positively associated with business performance measures.

#### *Multiple Continents*

Fang (2019) by means of a sample of 710 listed banks from 60 countries over the period 1997–2012 shows that foreign ownership is significantly associated with greater (lower) informativeness (synchronicity) in bank stock prices.

**Table 3.23** Gender diversity and accounting quality in banks

| n. | Year | Authors | Journal | Geographic area | Specific country | Sample | Listed/ unlisted | Sample period | Year (sample) | | Gender variables | Earnings management |
|---|---|---|---|---|---|---|---|---|---|---|---|---|
| 1 | 2017 | García-Sánchez I.-M., Martínez-Ferrero J., García-Meca E. | *Management Decision* | Multiple continents | | 159 | N/A | N/A | 2004 | 2010 | Prop. female directors | Positive |

Source: Authors constructed

**Table 3.24** Gender diversity and CEO power in banks

| n. | Year | Authors | Journal | Geographic area | Specific country | Sample | Listed/ unlisted | Sample period | Year (sample) | | Gender variables | Gender |
|---|---|---|---|---|---|---|---|---|---|---|---|---|
| 1 | 2017 | Ting H.-I., Chueh H., Chang P.-R. | *Emerging Markets Review* | Asian data | China | 140 | N/A | Mix | 1991 | 2011 | | 1 |

Source: Authors constructed

*African Data*

Bokpin (2013) using a sample of 148 banks in Ghana over the period 1999–2007 shows that banks with foreign ownership are more profitable and cost-efficient than domestic banks.

It is clear a positive relation between foreign ownership structure and banks' performance (Table 3.25).

The remaining researches have investigated the relation between foreign ownership and the following items: bank efficiency, risk, and CSR.

*Foreign Ownership Structure and Efficiency*

*African Data*

Adeabah et al. (2019) using a sample of 21 African commercial banks during the period 2009–2017 find that the foreign-owned banks are less efficient than local-owned ones.

Bokpin (2013) using a sample of 148 banks in Ghana over the period 1999–2007 shows that banks with foreign ownership are more profitable and cost-efficient than domestic banks.

In this case, the two results are in contrast (Table 3.26).

*Foreign Ownership Structure and Risk*

*Asian Data*

Yeh (2017) by means of a sample of 78 listed Japanese banks over the period 2007–2008 shows that foreign shareholders increase risk-taking activities in pursuit of higher returns.

Unfortunately, we have only one research in Asia that investigates the relation between foreign ownership and banks' risk-taking (Table 3.27).

The relation is negative; it means that foreign owners might increase the level of risk-taking. This could explain the higher performance founded in the previous articles that investigate the relation between foreign ownership and banks' performance. Unfortunately, only one research in Asia is available, so we cannot generalize our results.

*Foreign Ownership Structure and CSR*

*Asian Data*

Orazalin (2019) using a sample of 38 listed banks in Kazakhstan over the period 2010–2016 shows that banks with a foreign ownership disclose more transparent and extensive information on corporate social responsibility activities than banks owned by state and local investors.

Also, in this case, we have only one research in Asia that investigates the relation between foreign ownership and CSR (Table 3.28).

**Table 3.25** Foreign ownership structure and performance in banks

| n. | Year | Authors | Journal | Geographic area | Specific country | Sample | Listed/ unlisted | Type of banks | Period | | Type of ownership structure | Performance |
|---|---|---|---|---|---|---|---|---|---|---|---|---|
| 1 | 2020 | Rashid M.H.U., Zobair S.A.M., Chowdhury M.A.I., Islam A. | *Business Research* | Asian data | Bangladesh | 30 | Listed | N/A | 2003 | 2017 | Foreign ownership | Positive |
| 2 | 2013 | Chahal H., Kumari A. | *Corporate Governance (Bingley)* | Asian data | India | 1 | N/A | N/A | 1996 | 2007 | Foreign ownership | Positive |
| 3 | 2019 | Fang Y., Hasan I., Leung W.S., Wang Q. | *Journal of International Business Studies* | Multiple continents | Sixty countries | 710 | Listed | N/A | 1997 | 2012 | Foreign ownership | Positive |
| 4 | 2013 | Bokpin G.A. | *Corporate Governance (Bingley)* | Africa | Ghana | 148 | N/A | N/A | 1999 | 2007 | Foreign ownership | Positive |

Source: Authors constructed

**Table 3.26** Foreign ownership structure and cost-efficiency in banks

| n. | Year | Authors | Journal | Geographic area | Specific country | Sample | Listed/ unlisted | Type of banks | Period | | Type of ownership structure | Efficiency |
|---|---|---|---|---|---|---|---|---|---|---|---|---|
| 1 | 2019 | Adeabah D., Gyeke-Dako A., Andoh C. | *Corporate Governance (Bingley)* | Africa | | 21 | N/A | Commercial | 2009 | 2017 | Foreign ownership | Negative |
| 2 | 2013 | Bokpin G.A. | *Corporate Governance (Bingley)* | Africa | Ghana | 148 | N/A | N/A | 1999 | 2007 | Foreign ownership | Positive |

Source: Authors constructed

**Table 3.27** Foreign ownership structure and risk banks

| n. | Year | Authors | Journal | Geographic area | Specific country | Sample | Listed/unlisted | Type of banks | Period | | Type of ownership structure | Risk |
|---|---|---|---|---|---|---|---|---|---|---|---|---|
| 1 | 2017 | Yeh T.-M. | *Corporate Governance (Bingley)* | Asian data | Japan | 78 | Listed | N/A | 2007 | 2008 | Foreign ownership | Negative |

Source: Authors constructed

**Table 3.28** Foreign ownership structure and CSR in banks

| n. | Year | Authors | Journal | Geographic area | Specific country | Sample | Listed/ unlisted | Type of banks | Period | | Type of ownership structure | CSR |
|---|---|---|---|---|---|---|---|---|---|---|---|---|
| 1 | 2019 | Orazalin N. | *Corporate Governance (Bingley)* | Asian data | Kazakhstan | 38 | Listed | Commercial | 2010 | 2016 | Foreign ownership | Positive |

Source: Authors constructed

**Table 3.29** Main findings and suggestions for regulators and researchers (only clear relations are reported)

| | Suggestion for regulators | Agency aspects | Research |
|---|---|---|---|
| Foreign shareholders may impact positively on banks' performance | Incentivize participations from foreign shareholders | • Foreign shareholders improve monitoring. | • Research if the increase in performance is due to an increase in banks' risk-taking. |

Source: Authors constructed

We can observe that foreign shareholders in banks have a strong positive impact on different banks' characteristics. Unfortunately, the relation with banks' risk-taking and CSR activities has been studied only in two researches. Table 3.29 reports suggestions for regulators and researchers.

### Concentrated Ownership Structure

The last CG area examined is the role of the concentrated ownership structure. As we know, a concentrated ownership structure means that shareholders can monitor directly directors' behaviors eliminating the agency cost that arise between dispersed shareholders and directors (their goals are aligned, that is, maximizing bank's value). In this context, usually directors are selected from the majority shareholders. A typical case of concentrated ownership structure exists in family firms. In these firms, a family holds the majority of the stocks, and family members sit on the BOD (i.e., there is no separation between ownership and control). The concentrate ownership structure has been investigated in relation to two banks' aspects, that is, risk and compensation.

#### *Concentrated Ownership Structure and Risks*

##### *Multiple Continents*

Laeven and Levine (2009) find that the identical regulation affects banks' risk-taking in a different way depending on the banks' ownership structure. More powerful owners tend to take greater risk. They use a sample of 250 unlisted banks from multiple countries over the period 1996–2001.

Laeven (2002) using a sample of 144 listed banks from multiple continents over the period 1991–1998 finds that banks with concentrated ownership structures tend to increase their risk-taking.

##### *Asian Data*

Kim et al. (2007) by means of a sample of 198 Japanese banks studied over the period 1983–1996 find that in an era of less restrictive regulatory environment (i.e.,

1986–1988), there is a strong and positive correlation between concentrated ownership structure and risk. The authors describe this relation as a sign of increased oversight from shareholders during less restrictive regulatory environment. In fact, in these periods, shareholders can fully enjoy the (potential) payoff from their risk-taking. Hence, they increase their quota in banks to leverage on this freely enjoyable risk-taking period.

In these articles, we can observe a clear relation between concentrated ownership structure and an increase in banks' risk-taking (Table 3.30a). We can link this negative relation to our **second agency cost (depositors vs. shareholders and directors), that is**, when shareholders' and directors' goal is to maximize bank's value (their goals are aligned when the ownership structure is concentrated), they could have the incentive to increase bank's risk appetite because the main peril of a potential bank's failure is on depositors and only partially on them; at the opposite, the increase in expected returns makes only shareholders and directors wealthier.

*Concentrated Ownership Structure and Compensation*

*European Data*

Słomka-Gołębiowska and Urbanek (2016) utilizing a sample of 16 listed banks located in Poland (period 2005–2013) find that when the ownership structure is concentrated, there is not overcompensation of executive directors.

*Asian Data*

Luo (2015) by means of a sample of 210 Chinese banks in the period 2005–2012 shows that ownership concentration reduces executive compensation in Chinese banking system.

We can observe that a concentrated ownership structure may ensure efficient monitoring function reducing directors' overcompensation (Table 3.30b).

Finally, we can observe that a concentrated ownership structure in the banking sector can increase banks' risk appetite. At the same time, the stronger monitoring on directors' behavior can reduce over compensation. Table 3.31 reports these findings.

Government-Owned Banks

The third type of ownership structure looks at government-owned banks.

*Government-Owned Banks and Risks*

*Multiple Continents*

Elamer (2019) exploiting a sample of 100 listed commercial banks located in Middle East and North Africa (MENA) countries (period 2006–2013) finds that governmental ownership has a positive effect on the level of risk disclosures by banks.

**Table 3.30a** Concentrated ownership structure and risks in banks

| n. | Year | Authors | Journal | Geographic area | Specific country | Sample | Listed/ unlisted | Type of banks | Period | | Type of ownership structure | Risk |
|---|---|---|---|---|---|---|---|---|---|---|---|---|
| 1 | 2009 | Laeven L., Levine R. | *Journal of Financial Economics* | Multiple continents | | 250 | Unlisted | N/A | 1996 | 2001 | Concentrated ownership | Negative |
| 2 | 2002 | Laeven L. | *World Bank Economic Review* | Multiple continents | | 144 | Listed | N/A | 1991 | 1998 | Concentrated ownership | Negative |
| 3 | 2007 | Kim K.A., lee S.-H., Rhee S. G. | *Journal of Economics and Business* | Asian data | Japan | 198 | Mix | Commercial | 1983 | 1996 | Concentrated ownership | Negative |

Source: Authors constructed

**Table 3.30b** Concentrated ownership structure and compensation in banks

| n. | Year | Authors | Journal | Geographic area | Specific country | Sample | Listed/ unlisted | Type of banks | Period | | Type of ownership structure | Compensation (positive, reduction) |
|---|---|---|---|---|---|---|---|---|---|---|---|---|
| 1 | 2016 | Słomka-Gołębiowska A., Urbanek P. | *Emerging Markets Review* | EU data | Poland | 16 | Listed | N/A | 2005 | 2013 | Concentrated ownership | Positive |
| 2 | 2015 | Luo Y. | *Journal of Economics and Business* | Asian data | China | 210 | Listed | N/A | 2005 | 2012 | Concentrated ownership | Positive |

Source: Authors constructed

**Table 3.31** Main findings and suggestions for regulators and researchers (only clear relations are reported)

| | Suggestion for regulators | Agency aspects | Research |
|---|---|---|---|
| 1. A concentrated ownership structure may increase banks' risk-taking | When a bank ownership structure is concentrated, the supervisors should increase monitoring | • Shareholders and directors increase bank's risk-taking with the goal to maximize bank value. | • Investigating this relation. |
| | | (2° agency cost, that is, depositors vs. shareholders and directors) | |
| 2. A concentrated ownership structure reduces directors' overcompensation | | • Majority shareholders monitor directors' behaviors avoiding excessive compensation. | |

Dinç (2005) by means of a sample of 349 banks in the period 1994–2000 finds that banks in election years drastically increase their lending (and risk) in comparison to not government-owned banks.

*Government-Owned Banks and Compensation*

*Asian Data*

Luo (2015) by means of a sample of 210 Chinese banks in the period 2005–2012 shows state ownership negatively affects executive compensation in Chinese banking system.

Unfortunately, in this case, we have a limited number of articles available, and we cannot generalize our results.

### Directors' Stock Ownership

Bhagat and Bolton (2019) exploiting a sample of 100 US banks (period 2002–2006) find that directors' stock ownership is positively related to future performance.

Berger et al. (2016) using a sample of 341 commercial banks over the period 2007–2010 show that when lower-level managers (e.g., department heads or vice presidents) and non-CEO higher-level managers (e.g., COO and CFO) have more shareholdings, the probability of bank failure increases; in contrast, shareholdings of CEOs do not increase risk of failure.

Also in this case, we have mixed results and a limited amount of research.

| n. | Year | Authors | Journal | Geographic area | Specific country | Sample | Listed/ unlisted | Type of banks | Period | | Type of ownership structure | Risk |
|---|---|---|---|---|---|---|---|---|---|---|---|---|
| 1 | 2019 | Elamer A.A., Ntim C.G., Abdou H.A., Zalata A.M., Elmagrhi M. | *Accounting Forum* | Multiple continents | | 100 | Listed | Commercial | 2006 | 2013 | Government and family shareholdings | Positive (risk disclosure) |
| 2 | 2005 | Dinç I.S. | *Journal of Financial Economics* | Multiple continents | | 349 | N/A | N/A | 1994 | 2000 | Government ownership | Negative |

Source: Authors constructed

| n. | Year | Authors | Journal | Geographic area | Specific country | Sample | Listed/ unlisted | Type of banks | Period | | Type of ownership structure | Compensation (positive, reduction) |
|---|---|---|---|---|---|---|---|---|---|---|---|---|
| 1 | 2015 | Luo Y. | *Journal of Economics and Business* | Asian data | China | 210 | Listed | N/A | 2005 | 2012 | Government ownership | Positive |

Source: Authors constructed

| n. | Year | Authors | Journal | Geographic area | Specific country | Sample | Listed/ unlisted | Type of banks | Period | | Type of ownership structure | Performance |
|---|---|---|---|---|---|---|---|---|---|---|---|---|
| 1 | 2019 | Bhagat S., Bolton B. | *Journal of Corporate Finance* | US data | | 100 | N/A | N/A | 2002 | 2006 | Director's stock ownership | Positive |
| 2 | 2016 | Berger A.N., Imbierowicz B., Rauch C. | *Journal of Money, Credit and Banking* | US data | | 341 | N/A | Commercial | 2007 | 2010 | Director's stock ownership | Mixed |

Source: Authors constructed

### 3.1.5 Conclusions

As we can observe in this literature review, the number of articles that investigate CGBS constructs is still too small. We have to consider that we analyzed only articles published on the most relevant scientific journals in the world. These journals have a very high-quality revision process and select (usually) the best research articles.[20]

Here below are reported the main findings of this literature review:

(a) Increasing the proportion of independent directors can amplify banks' risk appetite. This is particularly true, in large and international banks, when there is a one-tier board and when independent directors have financial expertise.
(b) CEO duality, usually considered as a signal of poor CG quality, can instead reduce (not always) banks' risk appetite.
(c) In China and in the United States, increasing the proportion of women sitting on the board can reduce banks' risk appetite. In Europe, we have mixed or negative results.
(d) Gender diversity is positively correlated with the level of CSR disclosure.
(e) Gender diversity can mitigate directors' excessive compensation.
(f) The presence of foreign shareholders can improve banks' performance.
(g) The presence of foreign shareholders can improve banks' CSR disclosure.
(h) A concentrated ownership structure can increase banks' risk appetite.
(i) A concentrated ownership structure can mitigate excessive compensation.

## References

Adams RB, Ferreira D (2007) A theory of friendly boards. J Financ 62:217–250. https://doi.org/10.1111/j.1540-6261.2007.01206.x

Adams B, Ferreira D (2009) Women in the boardroom and their impact on governance and performance. J Financ Econ 94:291–309

Adams RB, Ferreira D (2012) Regulatory pressure and bank directors' incentives to attend board meetings, Renee Adams and Daniel Ferreira. Int Rev Financ 12(2):227–248

Adeabah D, Gyeke-Dako A, Andoh C (2019) Board gender diversity, corporate governance and bank efficiency in Ghana: a two stage data envelope analysis (DEA) approach. Corp Gov 19(2):299–320. https://doi.org/10.1108/CG-08-2017-0171

Ahern KR, Dittmar AK (2012) The changing of the boards: the impact on firm valuation of mandated female board representation. Q J Econ 127(1):137–197

Aljughaiman AA, Salama A (2019) Do banks effectively manage their risks? The role of risk governance in the MENA region. J Account Public Policy 38(5):106680. ISSN 0278-4254. https://doi.org/10.1016/j.jaccpubpol.2019.106680

Anderson CA, Anthony RN (1986) The new corporate directors. Insights for board member & executives. Wiley, New York

[20]The Q1 Scimago covers 381 scientific journals. Hence, the number of scientific journals cannot be considered small.

Andres A, Vallelado E (2008) Corporate governance in banking: the role of the Board of Directors. J Bank Financ 32(12):2570–2580. Available at SSRN: https://ssrn.com/abstract=1314877
Basel Committee on Banking Supervision (BCBS) (2015) Bank for international settlements, guidelines: corporate governance principles for banks
Basiruddin R, Ahmed H (2020) Corporate governance and Shariah non-compliant risk in Islamic banks: evidence from Southeast Asia. Corp Gov 20(2):240–262. https://doi.org/10.1108/CG-05-2019-0138
Ben Bouheni F, Cheffou A, Jawadi F (2018) Analyzing the governance structure of French banking groups. Res Int Bus Financ 44:40–48. ISSN 0275-5319. https://doi.org/10.1016/j.ribaf.2017.05.016
Berger AN, Kick T, Schaeck K (2014) Executive board composition and bank risk taking. J Corp Financ 28:48–65. ISSN 0929-1199. https://doi.org/10.1016/j.jcorpfin.2013.11.006
Berger AN, Imbierowicz B, Rauch C (2016) The roles of corporate governance in bank failures during the recent financial crisis. J Money Credit Bank 48(4):729–770
Berger A, Klapper L, Turk-Ariss R (2009) Bank competition and financial stability. Journal of Financial Services Research, Springer; Western Finance Association 35(2):99–118
BIS (2006) Enhancing corporate governance for banking organisations. Basel Committee Publications No. 122, February
Bhagat S, Bolton B (2019) Corporate governance and firm performance: the sequel. J Corp Financ 58:142–168. ISSN 0929-1199. https://doi.org/10.1016/j.jcorpfin.2019.04.006
Birindelli G, Iannuzzi AP, Savioli M (2019) The impact of women leaders on environmental performance: evidence on gender diversity in banks. Corp Soc Resp Environ Manag 26: 1485–1499. https://doi.org/10.1002/csr.1762
Birindelli G, Chiappini H, Savioli M (2020) When do women on board of directors reduce bank risk? Corp Gov 20(7):1307–1327. https://doi.org/10.1108/CG-03-2020-0089
Bokpin GA (2013) Ownership structure, corporate governance and bank efficiency: an empirical analysis of panel data from the banking industry in Ghana. Corp Gov 13(3):274–287. https://doi.org/10.1108/CG-05-2010-0041
Brewster C, Wood G, Brookes M (2008) Similarity, isomorphism or duality? Recent survey evidence on the human resource management policies of multinational corporations. Br J Manag 19(4):320–342 https://ssrn.com/abstract=1297546 or doi:https://doi.org/10.1111/j.1467-8551.2007.00546.x
Campbell K, Minguez-Vera A (2008) Gender diversity in the boardroom and firm financial performance. J Bus Ethics 83(3):435–451
Cardillo G, Onali E, Torluccio G (2020) Does gender diversity on banks' boards matter? Evidence from public bailouts. J Corp Financ 71:101560. ISSN 0929-1199. https://doi.org/10.1016/j.jcorpfin.2020.101560
Caspar R (2007) Does female board representation influence firm performance? The Danish evidence. Corp Govern Int Rev 15(2):404–413
Chahal H, Kumari A (2013) Examining talent management using CG as proxy measure: a case study of State Bank of India. Corp Gov 13(2):198–207. https://doi.org/10.1108/14720701311316670
Daily CM, Dalton DR (1994) Bankruptcy and corporate governance: the impact of board composition and structure. Acad Manag J 37(6):1603–1617. https://doi.org/10.2307/256801
de Cabo RM, Gimeno R, Nieto MJ (2012) Gender diversity on European banks' boards of directors. J Bus Ethics 109(2):145–162. http://www.jstor.org/stable/23259307
De Vita G, Luo Y (2018) When do regulations matter for bank risk-taking? An analysis of the interaction between external regulation and board characteristics. Corp Gov 18(3):440–461. https://doi.org/10.1108/CG-10-2017-0253
Dinç IS (2005) 2005 politicians and banks: political influences on government-owned banks in emerging markets. J Financ Econ 77(2):453–479., ISSN 0304-405X. https://doi.org/10.1016/j.jfineco.2004.06.011

Directive 2013/36/EU of the European Parliament and of the Council of 26 June 2013 on access to the activity of credit institutions and the prudential supervision of credit institutions and investment firms, amending Directive 2002/87/EC and repealing Directives 2006/48/EC and 2006/49/EC Text with EEA relevance

Dodd-Frank Wall Street Reform and Consumer Protection Act of 2010

Dong Y, Girardone C, Kuo J-M (2017) Governance, efficiency and risk taking in Chinese banking. Br Acc Rev 49(2):211–229. ISSN 0890-8389. https://doi.org/10.1016/j.bar.2016.08.001

Dowling J, Pfeffer J (1975) Organizational legitimacy: social values and organizational behavior. Pac Sociol Rev 18(1):122–136. https://doi.org/10.2307/1388226

Elamer AA, Ntim CG, Abdou HA, Zalata AM, Elmagrhi M (2019) The impact of multi-layer governance on bank risk disclosure in emerging markets: the case of Middle East and North Africa. Acc Forum 43(2):246–281

Erhardt NL, Werbel JD, Shrader CB (2003) Board of director diversity and firm financial performance. Corp Gov 11:102–111

Fama EF, Jensen MC (1983) Separation of ownership and control. J Law Econ 26:301–326

Fang Y, Hasan I, Leung WS et al (2019) Foreign ownership, bank information environments, and the international mobility of corporate governance. J Int Bus Stud 50:1566–1593. https://doi.org/10.1057/s41267-019-00240-w

Farrell K, Hersch P (2005) Additions to corporate boards: the effect of gender. J Corp Financ 11(1–2):85–106

Ferris GR, Blass F, Douglas C, Kolodinsky R, Treadway D (2003) Personal reputation in organizations. In: Organizational behavior: the state of the science. Lawrence Erlbaum, Mahwah, pp 211–246

Francoeur C, Labelle R, Sinclair-Desagné B (2008) Gender diversity in corporate governance and top management. J Bus Ethics 81(1):83–95

García-Meca E (2016) Political connections, gender diversity and compensation policy. Rev Manag Sci 10:553–576

García-Sánchez I-M, Martínez-Ferrero J, García-Meca E (2017) Gender diversity, financial expertise and its effects on accounting quality. Manag Decis 55(2):347–382. https://doi.org/10.1108/MD-02-2016-0090

Gregory-Smith I, Main B, O'Reilly C (2014) Appointments, pay and performance in UK boardrooms by gender. Econ J 124(574):F109–F128

Harkin SM, Mare DS, Crook JN (2020) Independence in bank governance structure: empirical evidence of effects on bank risk and performance. Res Int Bus Financ 52(C)

Hermalin BE, Weisbach MS (2003) Boards of Directors as an endogenously determined institution: a survey of the economic literature. Econ Policy Rev 9(1). Available at SSRN: https://ssrn.com/abstract=794804

Huse M (2005) Accountability and creating accountability: a framework for exploring behavioural perspectives of corporate governance. Br J Manag 16:S65–S79. https://doi.org/10.1111/j.1467-8551.2005.00448.x

Iselin M (2020) Estimating the potential impact of requiring a stand-alone board-level risk committee. J Account Public Policy 39(5):106709. https://doi.org/10.1016/j.jaccpubpol.2019.106709

Jensen MC (1993) The modern industrial revolution, exit, and the failure of internal control systems. J Financ 48:831–880. https://doi.org/10.1111/j.1540-6261.1993.tb04022.x

Johnson JL, Ellstrand AE, Daily CM (1996) Board of directors: a review and research agenda. J Manag 22:409–438

Joy L, Carter NM, Wagner HM, Narayanan S (2007) The bottom line: corporate performance and women's representation on boards. Catalyst. http://www.catalyst.org/system/files/The_Bottom_Line_Corporate_Performance_and_Womens_Representation_on_Boards.pdf

Kiliç M, Kuzey C, Uyar A (2015) The impact of ownership and board structure on Corporate Social Responsibility (CSR) reporting in the Turkish banking industry. Corp Gov 15(3):357–374. https://doi.org/10.1108/CG-02-2014-0022

Kim KA, Kitsabunnarat-Chatjuthamard P, Nofsinger JR (2007) Large shareholders, board independence, and minority shareholder rights: evidence from Europe. J Corp Finan 13(5):859–880
Kusi BA, Gyeke-Dako A, Agbloyor EK, Darku AB (2018) Does corporate governance structures promote shareholders or stakeholders value maximization? Evidence from African banks. Corp Gov 18(2):270–288. https://doi.org/10.1108/CG-09-2016-0177
Laeven L (2002) Bank risk and deposit insurance. World Bank. © World Bank. https://openknowledge.worldbank.org/handle/10986/17187 License: CC BY-NC-ND 3.0 IGO
Laeven L, Levine R (2009) Bank governance, regulation and risk taking. J Financ Econ 93(2): 259–275. ISSN 0304-405X. https://doi.org/10.1016/j.jfineco.2008.09.003
Lasfer MA (2006) The interrelationship between managerial ownership and board structure. J Bus Financ Acc 33:1006–1033. https://doi.org/10.1111/j.1468-5957.2006.00600.x
Lewellyn KB, Muller-Kahle MI (2012) CEO power and risk taking: evidence from the subprime lending industry. Corp Gov 20:289–307. https://doi.org/10.1111/j.1467-8683.2011.00903.x
Liu Y, Wei Z, Xie F (2014) Do women directors improve firm performance in China? J Corp Financ 28(C):169–184
Lu J, Boateng A (2018) Board composition, monitoring and credit risk: evidence from the UK banking industry. Rev Quant Finan Acc 51:1107–1128. https://doi.org/10.1007/s11156-017-0698-x
Lückerath-Rovers M (2013) Women on boards and firm performance. J Manag Gov 17(2):491–509
Luo Y (2015) CEO power, ownership structure and pay performance in Chinese banking. J Econ Bus 82:3–16. ISSN 0148-6195. https://doi.org/10.1016/j.jeconbus.2015.04.003
Mazzotta R, Ferraro O (2020) Does the gender quota law affect bank performances? Evidence from Italy. Corp Gov 20(6):1135–1158. https://doi.org/10.1108/CG-08-2019-0252
Minton B, Taillard J, Williamson R (2014) Financial expertise of the board, risk taking, and performance: evidence from bank holding companies. J Financ Quant Anal 49(2):351–380. https://doi.org/10.1017/S0022109014000283
Neifar S, Jarboui A (2018) Corporate governance and operational risk voluntary disclosure: evidence from Islamic banks. Res Int Bus Financ 46:43–54. ISSN 0275-5319. https://doi.org/10.1016/j.ribaf.2017.09.006
Nguyen DD, Hagendorff J, Eshraghi A (2015) Which executive characteristics create value in banking? Evidence from appointment announcements. Corp Gov 23:112–128. https://doi.org/10.1111/corg.12084
Orazalin N (2019) Corporate governance and corporate social responsibility (CSR) disclosure in an emerging economy: evidence from commercial banks of Kazakhstan. Corp Gov 19(3):490–507. https://doi.org/10.1108/CG-09-2018-0290
Palvia A, Vähämaa E, Vähämaa S (2015) Are female CEOs and chairwomen more conservative and risk averse? Evidence from the banking industry during the financial crisis. J Bus Ethics 131:577–594. https://doi.org/10.1007/s10551-014-2288-3
Palvia A, Vähämaa E, Vähämaa S (2020) Female leadership and bank risk-taking: evidence from the effects of real estate shocks on bank lending performance and default risk. J Bus Res 117: 897–909. ISSN 0148-2963. https://doi.org/10.1016/j.jbusres.2020.04.057
Pfeffer J, Salancik GR (1978) The external control of organizations: a resource dependence perspective. University of Illinois at Urbana-Champaign's Academy for Entrepreneurial Leadership Historical Research Reference in Entrepreneurship. Available at SSRN: https://ssrn.com/abstract=1496213
Proença C, Augusto M, Murteira J (2020) Political connections and banking performance: the moderating effect of gender diversity. Corp Gov 20(6):1001–1028. https://doi.org/10.1108/CG-01-2020-0018
Ramly Z, Chan SG, Mustapha MZ et al (2017) Women on boards and bank efficiency in ASEAN-5: the moderating role of the independent directors. Rev Manag Sci 11:225–250. https://doi.org/10.1007/s11846-015-0186-4
Rashid MH, Zobair SAM, Chowdhury MAI, Islam A (2020) Corporate governance and banks' productivity: evidence from the banking industry in Bangladesh. Bus Res 13(2):615–637

Słomka-Gołębiowska A, Urbanek P (2016) Corporate boards, large blockholders and executive compensation in banks: evidence from Poland. Emerg Mark Rev 28:203–220. ISSN 1566-0141. https://doi.org/10.1016/j.ememar.2016.08.001

Stiles P, Taylor B (2001) Boards at work: how directors view their roles and responsibilities. Oxford University Press, Oxford

Tapver T, Laidroo L, Gurvitš-Suits NA (2020) Banks' CSR reporting—do women have a say? Corp Gov 20(4):639–651. https://doi.org/10.1108/CG-11-2019-0338

Ting H, Huang P (2018) CEOs' power and perks: evidence from Chinese banks. J Econ Bus 97:19–27. ISSN 0148-6195. https://doi.org/10.1016/j.jeconbus.2018.02.003

Ting H-I, Chueh H, Chang P-R (2017) CEO power and its effect on performance and governance: evidence from Chinese banks. Emerg Mark Rev 33(C):42–61

Vallascas F, Mollah S, Keasey K (2017) Does the impact of board independence on large bank risks change after the global financial crisis? J Corp Finan 44:149–166

Wang T, Hsu C (2013) Board composition and operational risk events of financial institutions. J Bank Financ 37(6):2042–2051. ISSN 0378-4266. https://doi.org/10.1016/j.jbankfin.2013.01.027

Yeh T-M (2017) Governance, risk-taking and default risk during the financial crisis: the evidence of Japanese regional banks. Corp Gov 17(2):212–229. https://doi.org/10.1108/CG-02-2016-0027

Zattoni A, Cuomo F (2010) How independent, competent and incentivized should non-executive directors be? An empirical investigation of good governance codes. Br J Manag 21:63–79. https://doi.org/10.1111/j.1467-8551.2009.00669.x

# Chapter 4
# CG Stock Markets and the Environmental, Social, and Corporate Governance (ESG) Indicators

## 4.1 How Corporate Governance Affects Stock Markets

If the empirical analysis testifies that governance has an undoubtful impact on stock price, we then examined how this correlation is used by the investment industry. On this aspect, ESG[1] indexes, which incorporate governance aspects as key criteria, are becoming increasingly popular benchmarks. We investigated the nature of the five blocks composing the pillars of the governance criteria within the main ESG indexes.

They are board effectiveness, stakeholder governance, governance ethics, governance disclosure, and shareholders' rights. Each of these provisions has several sub-provisions. The rational of their inclusion in the indexes laid mainly on the empirical evidence of their relevance. There is now a consolidated literature highlighting the importance of these factors. The attention to governance factors activated a significant amount of regulation on the topic. Regulatory framework infrastructure is now immense. However, governance scandals have not diminished, suggesting that even if the governance infrastructure was adequate, the board and management behavior sometimes were inadequate. A perfect infrastructure could help to maintain a good governance, but after all, banks are made by human being with their biases.

[1]Environmental, social, and corporate governance.



B. Buchetti, A. Santoni, *Corporate Governance in the Banking Sector*, Contributions to Finance and Accounting, https://doi.org/10.1007/978-3-030-97575-3_4

### 4.1.1 *Influence of Corporate Governance on Stock Performance*

Weak corporate governance in the banking industry is often identified as one of the causes of the global crisis[2] (Saghi-Zedek and Tarazi 2015) between the mid-2007 and early 2009. The US Financial Crisis Commission on its final report concluded that "dramatic failures of corporate governance and risk management at many systemically financial institutions were a key cause of this crisis."[3]

Gompers et al. (2003)[4] demonstrated empirically the quantitative impact of a weak corporate governance. Using the incidence of 24 governance rules, they constructed a "governance index" to proxy for the level of shareholder's rights at about 1500 large firms during the 1990s. They found that firms with stronger shareholder's rights (considered a proxy of a good governance) had higher firm value, higher profits, higher sales growth, and lower capital expenditures and made fewer corporate acquisitions. Their analysis showed an earned abnormal return of 8.5% from an investment strategy based on buying firms in the lowest decile of the index (strongest rights) and selling firms in the highest decile of the index (weakest rights) (see Footnote 4).

There is a vast literature exploring the governance impact on the company performances (Fernandes et al. 2018)[5] and as such on the stock performances. We will review in this chapter the main conclusions of the academic specifically on the stock performance angle.

Academic research considers four different relationships between stock performance and corporate governance (see Fig. 4.1).

The first is the relationship between ownership concentration and stock prices, and the second is the relationship between board of directors and financial performance. Another aspect we investigated is the relationship between executive compensation and stock prices. And the lastly is the relationship between executive management and stock prices.

Oswald and Jahera (1991)[6] evaluated the relationship between ownership concentration and the stock returns and concluded that concentrated ownership positively indeed affects the stock performance of a firm. Their analysis suggests that

---

[2]Saghi-Zedek, N. and Tarazi, A. (2015) Excess control rights, financial crisis and bank profitability and risk. Journal of Banking & Finance 55: 361–79.

[3]United States Financial Crisis Inquiry Commission (2011), The financial crisis inquiry report: Final report of the national commission on the causes of the financial and economic crisis in the United States, January, https://www.gpo.gov/fdsys/pkg/GPO-FCIC/pdf/GPO-FCIC.pdf, accessed 21 July 2016.

[4]Paul Gompers & Joy Ishii & Andrew Metrick, 2003. "Corporate Governance and Equity Prices," The Quarterly Journal of Economics, MIT.

[5]Catarina Fernandes et al. Bank Governance and Performance: A Survey of the Literature. Journal of Banking Regulation July 2018.

[6]Oswald, S. L., & Jahera Jr., J. S. (1991). The influence of ownership on performance: An empirical study. Strategic Management Journal, 12(4), 321–326.

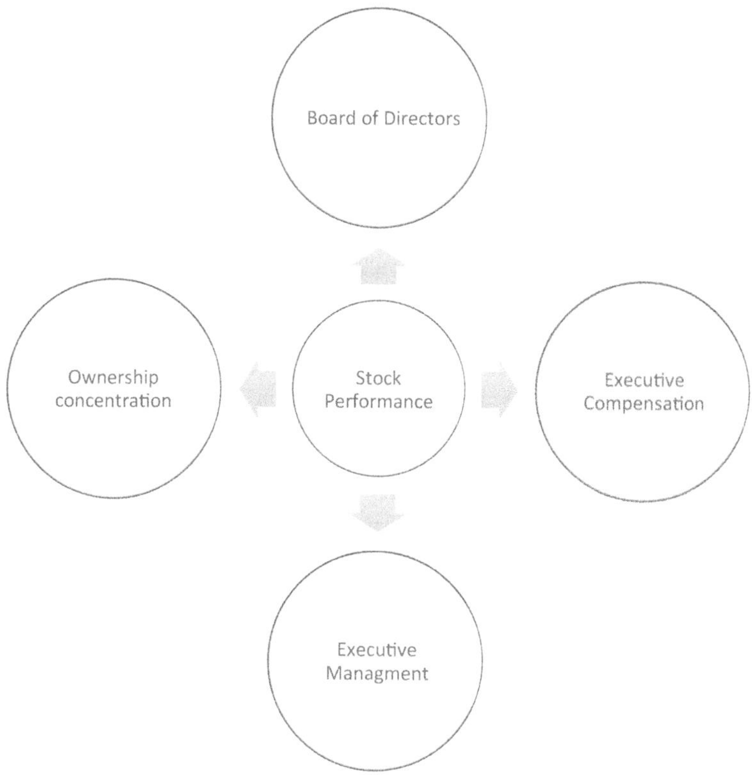


**Fig. 4.1** Stock price performances and corporate governance relation

large shareholders play an active role in influencing the decisions of the management, thus inducing it to act in the best interest of the shareholders. This in turn has a positive impact on the stock performance of the company (Lima and Hossain 2018).[7] Similarly, Chen[8] reports an overall positive relationship between ownership concentration and stock performance of a company. Explicit positive relationship was observed in the case of top management ownership and domestic ownership with relations to the stock prices.

Hopper Wruck (1989)[9] analyzed the empirical link between the market response to corporate financing decisions, as private sales of equity, and changes in ownership concentration (defined here as the percentage holdings of the largest shareholders as

[7]Lima, M. M., & Hossain, M. M. (2018). Ownership structure and firm performance: Testing monitoring and expropriation hypotheses for Bangladeshi companies. Journal of Finance and Banking, 14(1–2), 1–21.

[8]Jian Chen. Ownership Structure as Corporate Governance Mechanism: Evidence from Chinese Listed Companies. Economics of Planning volume 34, pages 53–72(2001).

[9]Karen Hopper Wruck. Equity ownership concentration and firm value: Evidence from private equity financings. Journal of Financial Economics. Volume 23, Issue 1, June 1989, Pages 3–2.

reported in the proxy statements). Against previous analyses, Wruck suggests that the announcement of a private sale of equity increases shareholder's wealth by 4.5% on average. The effect depends on the resulting level of ownership concentration and the purchaser's current or anticipated relationship with the firm. He distinguishes two ranges: when the level of ownership concentration after the sale is low (0–5%), the relation between changes in firm value at announcement and changes in ownership concentration is positive. On the other side, with an initial level of ownership concentration between 5% and 25%, the impact is negative. In this range, apparently, the ability of incumbent shareholders to become entrenched outweighs any benefits of having a blockholder in place.

Hu and Izumida (2008)[10] analyzed a panel of manufacturing firms listed on the first section of the Tokyo Stock Exchange from 1980 through 2005. They found that ownership concentration has a significant effect on current and future corporate performance. They found confirmation in their analysis of the U-shaped relation of concentration to performance as suggested by Wruck. They also highlighted differences between countries and stock markets. The literature based on the United States shows that corporate performance is a determinant of ownership structure, but not vice versa. In contrast, "significant parts around the world, including many Asian, European, and Latin American countries, are categorized as having an internal control system of corporate governance, namely, a concentrated ownership structure and the narrower and less efficient securities markets. Ownership structure is likely to play a more important role in disciplining management and determining performance for the lack of effective external control mechanisms" (see Footnote 10).

Edwards and Weichenrieder (2004)[11] concentrated their analysis on the German market and found that the presence of a controlling shareholder in a German company can be beneficial, or at least not harmful, for minority shareholders provided that such a shareholder has cash flow rights in line with control rights.

The second most frequently analyzed relationship by researchers is the one between the board of directors and corporate performances among which stock prices. The conclusions have been not homogenous even if the consensus seems confirming the correlation.

For example, several academic papers that analyzed the relationship between board independence and financial ratios as return on assets (ROA) or return on equity (ROE) found a positive relationship (e.g., Bonn (2004)[12] and Hutchinson and Gul (2002)).[13] Other studies have examined the relationship between board

[10]Hu, Y., & Izumida, S. (2008). The relationship between ownership and performance: A review of theory and evidence. International Business Research, 1(4), 72–81.

[11]Edwards, Jeremy S. S.; Weichenrieder, Alfons J. (2004): Ownership Concentration and Share Valuation, German Economic Review 5, S. 143–171.

[12]Bonn, I., 2004. Board structure and firm performance: Evidence from Australia. Journal of Management & Organization, 10(01), pp.14–24.

[13]Hutchinson, M. and Gul, F.A., 2002. Investment opportunities and leverage: some Australian evidence on the role of board monitoring and director equity ownership. Managerial finance, 28(3), pp. 19–36.

independence and valuation multiples as price-to-book ratios and provide some evidence of a positive and statistically significant relationship [e.g., Henry (2008)[14]].

De Andres and Vallelado (2008)[15] claim that an inverted "U"-shaped relationship exists between the board size and the bank's performance which suggests that with an increase in board members, the bank's performance increases but only until a certain level after which there is a steep decline in bank's performance. Such a behavior can be explained by considering the trade-offs between the advising and the controlling functions of the board.

Frino (2016)[16] examined for the Australian market the relationship between the proportion of independent directors on boards and company performance. "The results suggest that companies with balanced boards outperform all others in terms of market-adjusted stock price returns. Those with boards which are comprised of between 30 and 60% of board members who are independent outperform all others, with the evidence strongest for companies in the 40–60% category" (see Footnote 16).

The third relationship analyzed is the one between the executive compensation and stock prices. Academics are not united on confirming the possible relation between CEO compensation and stock performance.

Gong shows that both aggregate nominal and aggregate-realized CEO pay are significantly and positively related to aggregate market value changes and cumulative abnormal stock returns over CEO tenure. In contrast to Gong, other studies find that executive compensation has an insignificant or negative effect on stock performance. For instance, Larcker finds that there could be, statistically, a negative or positive association between executive stock option grants and operating performance, depending on the econometric models used. Cooper et al. conducting empirical research based on a broad cross section of executive compensation of S&P 1500 firms over the period 1994–2015 found that industry- and size-adjusted CEO pay is negatively related to future abnormal stock returns.

Mehran (1995)[17] examines the relationship between the structure of executive compensation and firm performance. The study's findings showed that firm performance was positively related to the percentage of executive compensation when this is an equity-based and that firm performance is positively related to the percentage of equity held by managers (Mehran 1995). This evidence advocates for incentive compensation and "suggests that the form rather than the level of compensation is what motivates managers to increase firm value" (see Footnote 17).

---

[14] Henry, D., 2008. Corporate governance structure and the valuation of Australian firms: Is there value in ticking the boxes? Journal of Business Finance & Accounting, 35(7–8), pp. 912–942.

[15] De Andres, P., & Vallelado, E. (2008). Corporate governance in banking: The role of the board of directors. Journal of banking & finance, 32(12), 2570–2580.

[16] Alex Frino (2016). The relationship between board independence and stock price performance. Australian Institute.

[17] Mehran, H. (1995). Executive compensation structure, ownership, and firm performance. Journal of financial economics, 38(2), 163–184.

The fourth relationship examined is the relation of executive management and stock performance.

With executive management style and strategies, we include the cumulative actions, policy, and strategy of the CEO, CFO, COO, and higher positions. Executive management style and decisions heavily influence a company's performance and can thus push a higher or lower company's stock price.

Malmendier and Tate (2015)[18] investigated the role of CEO behavior and one of the most common human bias the overconfidence. Among the most common approaches to measuring CEO overconfidence has been the approach toward company stock options. Overconfident CEOs tend to overweigh them in their portfolio that appears under diversified. Otto (2014)[19] suggests managerial forecasts of earnings as a possible lens through which researchers can observe overconfident beliefs. Malmendier and Tate (2015) also used portrayal in the business press to measure CEO beliefs. They count past articles in prominent business publications that refer to CEOs using words that suggest overconfidence ("confident"/"confidence," "optimistic"/"optimism") relative to the number of articles that refer to CEOs with words that are unlikely to suggest overconfidence ("cautious," "conservative," "practical," "reliable," and "steady").

Overconfidence and taking good stock performance for granted can hurt a company's stock market performance in different ways: from one side, an overconfident manager believes that the company's current assets are undervalued by the market; on the other side, an overconfident manager overestimates the value of future potential investments he or she might pick (see Footnote 18). Both approaches bring often to negative long-term stock performances.

Differently, Coughlan and Schmidt highlighted the inverse relation between management turnover and stock performance.[20] Warner et al. (1988)[21] studied the association between a firm's stock returns and subsequent top management changes. Consistent with internal monitoring of management, they found an inverse relation between the probability of a management change and a firm's share performance. In addition, stability among the executive management is critical to share performance: frequent executive changes can undermine a stock. Indeed, Warner et al. (1988)[22] found a reverse correlation between the probability of management change and stock price performance.

---

[18] Malmendier, U., & Tate, G. (2015). Behavioral CEOs: The role of managerial overconfidence. Journal of Economic Perspectives, 29(4), 37–60.

[19] Otto, C. A. (2014). CEO optimism and incentive compensation. Journal of Financial Economics, 114(2), pp.366–404.

[20] A.T. Coughlan and R.M. Schmidt. Compensation, turnover and performance. Journal of Accounting and Economics 1986.

[21] Jerold B.Warner, Ross L.Watts and Karen H. Wruck. Stock prices and top management changes Journal of Financial Economics Volume 20, January–March 1988.

[22] Warner, J. B., Watts, R. L., & Wruck, K. H. (1988). Stock prices and top management changes. Journal of financial Economics, 20, 61–492.

In closing, an efficient (identified by a low turnover), humble, and market-friendly executive management style could influence a stock price positively. While not so market-oriented, an overconfident executive management can have adverse effects and cause great loss of wealth of investors.

To summarize, in this paragraph, we examined the academic literature on a key topic as the influence of corporate governance on stock performance. The academic analysis concludes that there are various and very diverse findings on several parameters that might affect stock performance of companies. We highlighted four dimensions. First, the connection between ownership concentration and stock prices has been explored by various authors mostly founding generally a positive relation. The literature on the correlation between the board of directors and the stock performance of a company reveals mixed findings. There is a certain consensus on a positive relation, at least until a certain breaking point, which leads to a U-shaped relationship. The company's performance improves with the increase in board members until a certain level after which the performance worsens steeply. Another aspect we investigated is the relationship between executive compensation and stock prices. This is a still unclear topic. Still, we found literature suggesting a positive relation between cumulative nonstandard stock returns and CEO tenure. Literature tends to stress that the real manager's motivation comes from the form of the compensation (e.g., equity-based) rather than the level of it. The literature on the correlation between executive management and stock prices suggests that an efficient, excellent, and market-friendly executive management positively affects the stock performance.

## 4.2 Corporate Governance and the ESG Methodology

A survey conducted by McKinsey (2000)[23] asked to 200 international institutional investors how much they would pay more for the shares of a "well-governed company" than for those of a "poorly governed company" with comparable financial performance. The average premium among the most industrialized countries was about 20%. The companies with the largest "corporate governance discounts" were Korean and Italian companies, where investors would pay a 4% and 2% additional premium, respectively. The country with the smallest "corporate governance discounts" was the UK (3% lower than the average), besides Switzerland and Sweden. In this chapter, we investigate how governance is becoming a real concrete investment factor with the ESG[24] indexes that incorporate the governance aspects as key criteria, becoming increasingly popular benchmarks. Core of our analysis will be the factors, associated with governance, that are incorporated in the indexes.

---

[23] McKinsey, 2000: Investor Opinion Survey June 2000. London: McKinsey & Company.

[24] Environmental, social, and corporate governance.

**Fig. 4.2** ESG-G factors

According to a recent report by the OECD (2020),[25] the amount of professionally managed portfolios that have integrated key elements of ESG assessments exceeds USD 17.5 trillion globally. The number of open-ended funds and exchange-traded funds launched that use ESG criteria increased from 140 globally in 2012 to 564 in 2019. Several ESG providers include MSCI, Sustainalytics, Bloomberg, and Thomson Reuters.

Among the three components of the ESG acronym, the "G" aspect has indeed the longer history with governance index commonly used since the end of the last century. Among them, we can highlight the G-index by Gompers et al. (2003)[26] based on 24 governance provisions that weaken shareholder's rights and ranked companies based on their scores. A simplification of this index was developed by Bebchuk et al. (2009)[27] that reduced to six corporate governance provisions the one that can be associated with what is considered poor governance and that negatively affect valuation. The index was named "E-index" (E for entrenchment). Investigating the academic literature and the currently ESG market practice, we identified some recurring governance topics that can be divided in five blocks (see Fig. 4.2): board effectiveness, stakeholder governance, governance ethics, governance disclosure, and shareholders' rights. Each of these provisions has several sub-provisions.

Below we summarized the characteristics that make these provisions relevant for the criteria of good governance definition.

[25] ESG Investing: Practices, Progress and Challenges. OECD 2020.

[26] Gompers, P., Ishii, J., Metrick, A., 2003. Corporate governance and equity prices. Quarterly Journal of Economics 118, 107–155.

[27] Bebchuk, L., Cohen, A., Ferrell, A., 2009. What matters in corporate governance. Review of Financial Studies 22, 783–827.

## 4.3 Board Effectiveness

There is a wide literature advocating that the composition of a firm's board of directors can influence its environmental, social, and governance (ESG) ranking and therefore its performance. Several studies demonstrated that companies with high ESG ratings significantly outperform their counterparts in the stock market, demonstrating that there is strong positive relationship between a firm's sustainability performance and profitability.[28]

Several board's characteristics are taken into consideration to measure board effectiveness from the ESG point of view (see Fig. 4.3).

**Audit oversight.** The main task of an audit committees, separately chartered committee of the board of directors, is generally the oversight of the financial reporting process, the process of internal controls, and the audit. According to the NYSE listing guide,[29] firms must maintain audit committees with at least three directors, "all of whom have no relationship to the company that may interfere with the exercise of their independence from management and the company." The main characteristics of representative of the audit committees are the independent and the relevant expertise.

A study conducted by Klein (2000)[30] found a nonlinear negative relation between audit committee independence and earnings manipulation suggesting that it can help to prevent financial scandals.

**Board leadership.** Board leadership, defined as independent and effective, is a key component of good corporate governance and a key factor for a long-term value creation. Boards have the responsibility to influence CEOs to enhance the organization's approach to ESG and to good governance in general. Characteristics of an

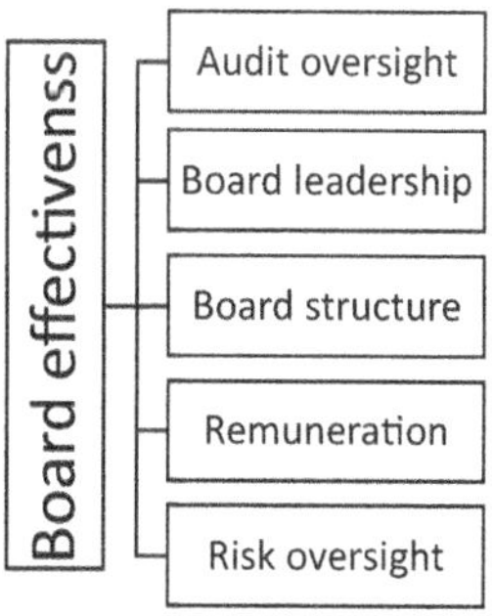


**Fig. 4.3** Board effectiveness

[28] Eccles, R.G.; Ioannou, I.; Serafeim, G. The Impact of Corporate Sustainability on Organizational Processes and Performance. Manag. Sci. 2014, 60, 2835–2857.

[29] NYSE Listing Guide, § 303.01(B)(2)(a).

[30] Klein, April, 2000a, CEO power, board independence and CEO compensation: An empirical investigation, working paper, New York University.

effective board leadership include among others time commitment to the tasks, good communicator, relevant industry expertise, integrity, and professional credibility. These factors allow a board member in general to be more independent from the CEO. April's[31] analysis suggests that when boards are more independent from the CEO, their effectiveness in monitoring the corporate financial accounting process increases.

**Board structure.** Among the most known ESG criteria used, on the governance side, there is the board structure. Particularly relevant are the dimension of the board, the gender, the age difference[32] among board members, and the balance of power between the CEO and the board of directors.[33]

Adams and Mehran found, for the period 1986–1996, on a random sample of 36 bank holding companies (BHCs) "no relation between firm performance and board composition and size once plausible sources of endogeneity are controlled for using firm fixed effects and potentially omitted variables related to M&A activity and organizational structure."[34] Relation changed significantly more recently. Pathan and Faff (2013), based on a sample of 212 large US BHCs over the period 1997–2011, highlighted a strong negative relation between bank board size and performance.[35] Increased complexity in the banking system, increased regulation, and significant volatility experienced more recently could explain part of this phenomenon. Another relevant board characteristic analyzed is the gender composition. There are many studies analyzing gender composition and the possible impact. One of the most extended is the one of Ali et al. (2020).[36] They applied a panel regression to examine the relationship between corporate governance and firms' financial performance. They used a sample of 3400 Shanghai stock exchange (SSE) listed firms, based on yearly observations from 2009 to 2018. Their results show that the "presence of female directors on the board is associated with improved firms' performance and that corporate social responsibility (CSR) moderates this relation, thus indicating that sharing strategic decision-making with female board

---

[31] Klein, April 1998, Firm performance and board committee structure, The Journal of Law & Economics 41, 275–303.

[32] Please refer to Chap. 3.

[33] Aguilera, Ruth et al., Corporate Governance and Social Responsibility; a comparative analysis of the UK and the US (Corporate Governance, Blackwell, Vol. 14, 2006).

[34] Renée B. Adams and Hamid Mehran, Corporate Performance, Board Structure, and Their Determinants in the Banking Industry Federal Reserve Bank of New York Staff Reports, no. 330 June 2008 JEL classification: G34, G21, J41, L22.

[35] Shams Pathan Robert Faff. Does board structure in banks really affect their performance? Journal of Banking & Finance Volume 37, Issue 5, May 2013, Pages 1573–1589.

[36] Rizwan Ali, Muhammad Safdar Sial, Talles Vianna Brugni, Jinsoo Hwang, Nguyen Vinh Khuong and Thai Hong Thuy Khanh (2019). Does CSR Moderate the Relationship between Corporate Governance and Chinese Firm's Financial Performance? Evidence from the Shanghai Stock Exchange (SSE) Firms.

members revealed a better relationship between CSR and firms' financial performance" (see Footnote 36).

**Remuneration.** Sustainalytics, an independent global provider of ESG and corporate governance research and ratings, assessed in 2020 that "only 9% of FTSE All World companies link executive pay to ESG criteria, most of which address occupational health and safety (OH&S) risks in the materials, energy, and utilities sectors."[37] Majority of these companies were based in Australia (20%), Canada (16%), and France (10%). From the governance, the two most common ESG criteria used are diversity and ethical conduct and compliance.

Looking at the company compensation reports, we can highlight different approaches in the way corporates link CEO remuneration to ESG factors. The less mature approach sees the absence of any indexation between ESG issues and CEO compensation. A slightly more mature approach highlights some links, but the company does not disclose the weight of ESG. A relatively more mature approach sees the link by the company of the weight of each ESG metric in the CEO's variable compensation. Finally, there are companies that tie part of its CEO's remuneration directly to its ESG objectives.

**Risk oversight.** The concept of risk oversight, another relevant sub-provision of board effectiveness, is different from risk management as the latter is mainly responsible for the management, while risk oversight is related to the board's supervision of the risk management processes and the overall frameworks.

Rating agency such as Moody's views a board of directors' risk oversight role as critical to the sound running of an institution—especially for financial institutions. Moody's highlights the boards' role in shaping a firm's risk appetite and ensures a proper risk management framework is in place.

**Stakeholder governance.** ESG criteria assigned a relevant weight to stakeholder's engagement in the decision process. Stakeholders' engagement varies from operational, managerial, as well as strategic issues while the degree of the power granted range from nonparticipation to co-decision-making. Among the most important subcomponents of the stakeholder governance, the most common are the one related to government, institutions, and union as illustrated in Fig. 4.4.

**Government relations.** Henisz et al. (2019)[38] estimated that the share of corporate profits at stake from external engagement varies from 25% to 30% for the pharmaceuticals and healthcare to 50% in banking, where consumer's protection and capital requirement provisions to avoid bail out are critical. The sectors where government subsidies are particularly relevant are the automotive, aerospace and defense, and

[37] Sustainalytics (a Morningstar company). The State of Pay: Executive Remuneration and ESG Metrics, 2020.

[38] Witold Henisz, Tim Koller, and Robin Nuttall. Five ways that ESG creates value, McKinsey Quarterly November 2019.

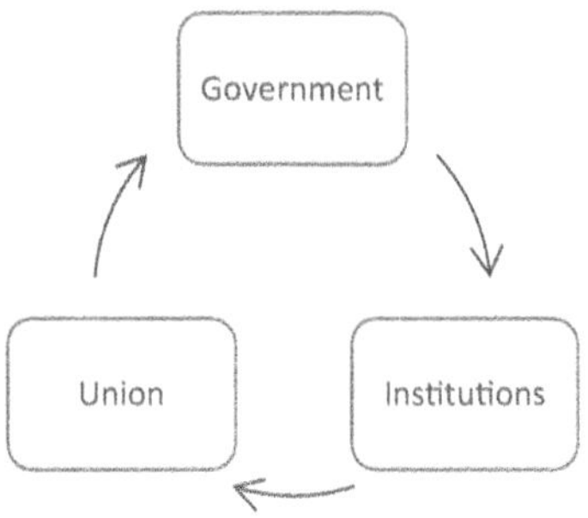


**Fig. 4.4** Stakeholder governance

tech sectors. According to Henisz et al. (2019), "a stronger external-value proposition can enable companies to achieve greater strategic freedom, easing regulatory pressure. In fact, in case after case across sectors and geographies, we've seen that strength in ESG helps reduce companies' risk of adverse government action. It can also engender government support" (see Footnote 38).

**Union relations.** Industrial relations are considered as key factors capable of addressing corporate and social responsibility issues. Bergeron et al. (2017)[39] study the role of management and trade union leadership and relations in Canada. "Based on a sample of 834 unionized workers, our results suggest that WRC (workplace relations climate) represents an important mechanism explaining the effect of the immediate supervisor's leadership in unionized settings. Results also show that transformational leadership on the part of union representatives is positively linked to union and organizational commitment" (see Footnote 39).

**Institutional relations.** Effective disclosure of information to shareholders concerning governance practices and financial issues has emerged as a clear need among investors. Investor relations communication is one of the communicative dimensions of shareholder orientation. Investor relations department is responsible for publishing financial reports, organizing road shows and analysts' meetings, and having one-to-one talks with institutional investors. Healy et al. (1999)[40] tested the stock performance of the 97 firms with 3-year consecutive increases in AIMR (Association for Investment Management and Research) disclosure ratings[41] in the 1990s and find that on average, these firms' stocks earned excess risk-adjusted returns of approximately 5% over this period.

**Governance ethics.** The exponential growth in the past 10 years of corporate scandals and failures has redirected attention to issues of ethics, trust, and

[39] C. Bergeron, O. Doucet, M. Hennebert. The Role of Management and Trade Union Leadership on Dual Commitment: The Mediating Effect of the Workplace Relations Climate, Wiley 2017.

[40] Association of Investment Management and Research (AIMR) surveys.

[41] Healy, P.M., Hutton, A.P. and Palepu, K.G. (1999), Stock Performance and Intermediation Changes Surrounding Sustained Increases in Disclosure, Contemporary Accounting Research, Vol. 16 No. 3, 486–520.

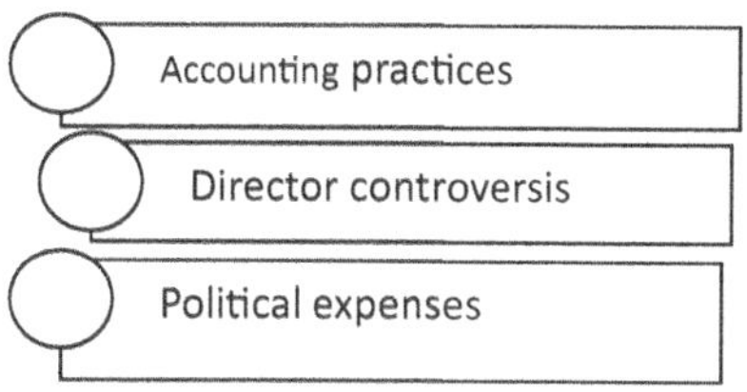


**Fig. 4.5** Governance ethics in the ESG methodologies

accountability as sign of good corporate governance. ESG methodologies usually consider among the most relevant one the accounting practices, controversies, and political expenses disclosure as illustrated in Fig. 4.5.

**Accounting practices.** Quality of financial statement and reported information is important to communicate corporate values to investors and to supervision. McLellan and Sherine (2013) analyzed the fit between the strategy employed and the management accounting practices adopted by an organization highlighting that "the more that the management accounting practices adopted by an organization are aligned with strategic objectives of that organization, the greater the business performance... findings indicate that a fit between the strategy employed and the management accounting practices adopted by an organization have a positive and significant effect on organizational performance."[42]

**Director controversies.** Given the growing focus on governance, supervisors are now taking further steps to enhance fit and proper supervision. ECB (European Central Bank), for example, assesses the fitness and propriety of new board members against the following five criteria:

1. Absence of conflicts of interest. Board members must be able to act independently when taking decisions.
2. Experience: The candidate should have theoretical and practical capabilities to assume a specific role in the bank.
3. Reputation: Candidate should have a clean criminal record and no history of administrative or fiscal irregularities. Pending legal proceedings are also considered.
4. Time commitment.
5. Collective suitability.[43]

**Political expenses.** Political spending disclosure is among the most controversial topics in the corporate governance debate. One of the most influencing asset

[42]McLellan & Sherine. Journal of Accounting – Business & Management vol. 20 no. 1 (2013).

[43]www.bankingsupervision.europa.eu/press/publications/newsletter/2018

**Fig. 4.6** Governance disclosure

managers in the world, BlackRock, in its 2019 voting guidelines,[44] clarified very clearly his position:

> *...presented with shareholder proposals requesting increased disclosure on corporate political activities, we may consider the political activities of that company and its peers, the existing level of disclosure, and our view regarding the associated risks. We generally believe that it is the duty of boards and management to determine the appropriate level of disclosure of all types of corporate activity, and we are generally not supportive of proposals that are overly prescriptive in nature. We may decide to support a shareholder proposal requesting additional reporting of corporate political activities where there seems to be either a significant potential threat or actual harm to shareholders' interests, and where we believe the company has not already provided shareholders with sufficient information to assess the company's management of the risk* (see Footnote 44).

**Governance disclosure.** Disclosure is an effective tool for improving investor's protection and particularly minority investors. Since 1992, more than 107 codes, including revisions of existing codes, have been introduced in 35 countries according to the European Corporate Governance Institute.[45] Studies focus their attention on the ESG, pay, tax, and CDP (carbon disclosure project) disclosure as among the most beneficial to characterize a good corporate governance as illustrated in Fig. 4.6.

**ESG disclosure.** Lopez de Silanes et al. (2019) found a "strong relationship between the extent of ESG disclosure and the quality of a firm's disclosure. Furthermore, found that ESG is correlated with decreased risk. This result suggests that firms with good ESG scores are simply disclosing more information".[46] On the similar tone Fatemia et al found that "ESG strengths increase firm value and that weaknesses decrease it.... But more importantly, we find that disclosure plays a crucial moderating role by mitigating the negative effect of weaknesses and attenuating the positive effect of strengths."[47]

---

[44] https://www.blackrock.com/corporate/literature/fact-sheet/blk-responsible-investment-guidelines-us.pdf

[45] European Corporate Governance Institute (www.ecgi.org).

[46] Lopez de Silanes, Florencio and McCahery, Joseph A. and Pudschedl, Paul C., ESG Performance and Disclosure: A Cross-Country Analysis (December 18, 2019). TILEC Discussion Paper No. DP2019-032, European Corporate Governance Institute - Law Working Paper No. 481/2019.

[47] Ali Fatemia, Martin Glaumb, Stefanie Kaiserc. ESG performance and firm value: The moderating role of disclosure. Global Finance Journal Volume 38, November 2018, Pages 45–64.

**Pay disclosure.** There is ample literature sustaining that mandated compensation disclosure strengthens corporate governance by providing a mechanism that enables shareholders to exert pressure on the board, if necessary. Contrary to the absence of mandated disclosure, CEO compensation is likely to be less performance-contingent among widely held firms than among closely held firms.[48]

A study from Walid Ben-Amar and Daniel Zeghal[49] (2011) documents a positive (negative) relation between firm size, growth opportunities (leverage), and the extent of executive compensation disclosure.

**Tax disclosure.** The depth and quality of tax disclosure is becoming an increasingly important theme. A recent UN report on principles of responsible investment (PRI) summarizes the outcomes of a 2017–2019 engagement project on corporate tax transparency.[50] The report aimed to increase awareness "within companies of investor concerns around aggressive corporate tax practices and expectations of responsible tax practice; improve company disclosures across tax policy, governance and financial reporting; and identify best practice" (see Footnote 50).

Tax avoidance if in the short term drives profits in the medium long term would bring to governance, reputational, and earnings risks for companies. "These tax practices could be subject to scrutiny by tax authorities and consequently result in unexpected reputational damage, litigation costs and penalties" (see Footnote 50).

**CDP (carbon disclosure project).** The attention on corporate disclosure of carbon emissions grew significantly in the past few years. Qiana and Schalteggerb (2017) analyzed the relation between the carbon disclosure and the potential influence on the improvement of carbon performance:[51]

> *Using a change analysis of Global 500 companies and their carbon emission and disclosure data released between 2008 and 2012, this study finds that the change in carbon disclosure levels is positively associated with a subsequent change in carbon performance. . .the study confirms that carbon disclosure motivates companies and creates an 'outside-in' driven effect for subsequent change and improvement in carbon performance* (see Footnote 51).

**Shareholders' rights.** At the base of the shareholders' rights, there is the feasibility to state rights when they are violated either through civil or criminal procedures. Investors need to be able to challenge management and auditors while both should be subject to legal responsibility.

---

[48] Brickley, J., R. Lease and C. Smith, 1994. "Corporate voting: Evidence from charter amendment proposals", Journal of Corporate Finance, Vol. Pages 1, 5–31.

[49] Walid Ben-Amar and Daniel Zeghal (2011) Board of directors' independence and executive compensation disclosure transparency Canadian evidence. Journal of Applied Accounting Research Volume: 5 Issue: 1, to Volume: 22 Issue: 1.

[50] https://www.unpri.org/governance-issues/advancing-tax-transpa

[51] Wei Qiana, Stefan Schalteggerb. Revisiting carbon disclosure and performance: Legitimacy and management views. The British Accounting Review Volume 49, Issue 4, July 2017, Pages 365–379.

According to the OECD definition,[52] shareholders' rights "entails the protection of shareholders and always maintaining investor confidence in way of ensuring the continuous inflow of needed capital. Equitable treatment of shareholders entails the equitable treatment of all equity investors, including minority shareholders while protection of stakeholders' rights entails the skillful consideration and balancing of the interests of all stakeholders, including employees, customers, partners, and the local community" (see Footnote 52).

Gompers et al. (2003)[53] based on 24 governance provisions that weaken shareholder's rights and ranked companies based on their scores analyzed the performance of 1500 US large firms during the 1990s. They found that an investment strategy based on a basket of long company with strongest rights and short firms with the weakest rights would have earned abnormal returns of 8.5% per year during the sample period. The fundamental rational at the base of the abnormal return are the higher profits, higher sales growth, lower capital expenditures, and higher M&A discipline that firms with stronger shareholder's rights had versus the weakest one.

On the other side, Jiraporn et al.[54] revealed an interesting inverse association between dividend payout and shareholder's rights, indicating that "firms pay higher dividends where shareholder rights are more suppressed." This is line with the research by La Porta et al. (2000),[55] which contends that "firms with weak shareholder rights need to establish a reputation for not exploiting shareholders. As a result, these firms pay dividends more generously than do firms with strong shareholder rights" (see Footnote 55).

What seems to suggest the research of Jiraporn and La Porta et al. (2000) is that dividends substitute for shareholder's rights and this could explain part of the abnormal return.

## 4.4 Are Banks Utilizing ESG Internally?

While investors are becoming increasingly influenced by ESG topics, banks are still building their internal know-how. A recent survey[56] by European Commission revealed the knowledge of banks' management and the integration of ESG methodology in their governance. The results are somehow mixed.

[52] OECD, Organization for Economic Cooperation and Development (1999).

[53] Gompers, P., Ishii, J., Metrick, A., 2003. Corporate governance and equity prices. Quarterly Journal of Economics 118, 107–155.

[54] Jiraporn, Pornsit and Ning, Yixi, Dividend Policy, Shareholder Rights, and Corporate Governance (September 18, 2006).

[55] R. La Porta, F. Lopez-de-Silanes, A. Shleifer, R.W. Vishny Agency problems and dividend policies around the world Journal of Finance, 55 (2000), pp. 1–33.

[56] Development of tools and mechanisms for the integration of environmental, social and governance (ESG) factors into the EU banking prudential framework and into banks' business strategies and investment policies. European Commission. 2000.

Out of 42 banks (of which 29 from EU member states and 13 from non-EU member states), 25% of them reported having dedicated ESG risk committees and 13% having a dedicated committee at board level. Where dedicated committees are not in place, ESG themes are often discussed also within other committees. On the other hand, in 8% of banks, part of the panel admitted that ESG risk is not yet integrated within any committee discussion.

The survey clearly highlighted that majority of the banks interviewed placed the E factor as the stronger focus compared to the S and G pillars.

On the other side, governance appears to be best known among the three pillars of the ESG indicator. Corporate behavior and business ethics were a key governance topic for 85% of the respondents, ownership control for 73%, and to a lesser extent board quality, effectiveness, and topics such as audit, tax, and risk management.

A recent study by Whelan (2021)[57] investigated the ESG's know-how of 1188 Fortune 100 board directors in the United States.

The results were not particularly positive with only 29% of board members that reported ESG credentials. A more granular analysis of the results shows that only 6% have governance experience and majority of the credentials of the board member were concentrated in the S factor clustered on diversity and to lesser extent to healthcare category. On the governance side, very few board members reported credentials on corruptions, transparency, ethics, and governance topics. This is surprising considering the relevance of governance credentials for a sector as banks.

The report tends to point the finger, for the generally poor ESG credentials to a generational issue mixed to a professional transitional phase. On the specific financial poor governance credentials, we believe the sector has still a significant gap to fill.

## 4.5 Conclusion

We investigated the nature of the five blocks composing the pillars of the governance criteria within the main ESG indexes. They are board effectiveness, stakeholder governance, governance ethics, governance disclosure, and shareholders' rights. Each of these provisions has several sub-provisions. The rational of their inclusion in the indexes laid mainly on the empirical evidence of their relevance. There is now a consolidated literature highlighting the importance of these factors. Certain overarching governance principles remain undisputedly valid: banks need a process of checks and balances at all levels, well-defined lines of responsibility, and effective risk management and controls within their organizational structure. At the same time, quality of disclosure, shareholders' rights, and quality of communication are

[57] U.S. Corporate Boards Suffer from Inadequate Expertise in Financially Material ESG Matters Tensie Whelan Professor & Director, NYU Stern Center for Sustainable Business NYU Stern Researchers: Jamie Friedland & Ellen Knuti. January 2021.

becoming increasingly important in identifying a good governance practice. All these elements are now encapsulated in the ESG rating and in the G element.

## References

Ali R, Sial MS, Brugni TV, Hwang J, Khuong NV, Khanh THT (2020) Does CSR moderate the relationship between corporate governance and Chinese firm's financial performance? Evidence from the Shanghai Stock Exchange (SSE) firms. Sustainability (Switzerland) 12(1):149

Bebchuk L, Cohen A, Ferrell A (2009) What matters in corporate governance. Rev Financ Stud 22: 783–827

Ben-Amar W, Zeghal D (2011) Board of directors' independence and executive compensation disclosure transparency Canadian evidence. J Appl Account Res 5(1)–22(1)

Bergeron, Doucet O, Hennebert M (2017) The role of management and trade union leadership on dual commitment: the mediating effect of the workplace relations climate. Wiley, New York

Bonn I (2004) Board structure and firm performance: evidence from Australia. J Manag Organ 10(01):14–24

De Andres P, Vallelado E (2008) Corporate governance in banking: the role of the board of directors. J Bank Financ 32(12):2570–2580

Edwards JSS, Weichenrieder AJ (2004) Ownership concentration and share valuation. Ger Econ Rev 5:143–171

Fernandes C et al (2018) Bank governance and performance: a survey of the literature. J Bank Regul 19(3):236–256

Frino A (2016) The relationship between board independence and stock price performance. Australian Institute, Canberra

Gompers P, Ishii J, Metrick A (2003) Corporate governance and equity prices. Q J Econ 118(1): 107–155

Healy PM, Hutton AP, Palepu KG (1999) Stock performance and intermediation changes surrounding sustained increases in disclosure. Contemp Account Res 16(3):486–520

Henisz W, Koller T, Nuttall R (2019) Five ways that ESG creates value. McKinsey & Company, Chicago

Henry D (2008) Corporate governance structure and the valuation of Australian firms: is there value in ticking the boxes? J Bus Financ Acc 35(7–8):912–942

Hu Y, Izumida S (2008) The relationship between ownership and performance: a review of theory and evidence. Int Bus Res 1(4):72–81

Hutchinson M, Gul FA (2002) Investment opportunities and leverage: some Australian evidence on the role of board monitoring and director equity ownership. Manag Financ 28(3):19–36

Klein (2000) CEO power, board independence and CEO compensation: an empirical investigation, working paper. New York University, New York

La Porta F, Lopez-de-Silanes A, Shleifer RW (2000) Vishny Agency problems and dividend policies around the world. J Financ 55:1–33

Lima MM, Hossain MM (2018) Ownership structure and firm performance: testing monitoring and expropriation hypotheses for Bangladeshi companies. J Financ Bank 14(1–2):1–21

Lopez de Silanes F, McCahery JA, Pudschedl PC (2019) ESG performance and disclosure: a cross-country analysis (December 18, 2019). TILEC discussion paper no. DP2019-032, European Corporate Governance Institute—law working paper no. 481/2019

Malmendier U, Tate G (2015) Behavioral CEOs: the role of managerial overconfidence. J Econ Perspect 29(4):37–60

McKinsey (2000) Investor opinion survey June 2000. McKinsey & Company, London

Mc-Lellan JD, Sherine FAA (2013) Strategy and management accounting practices alignment and its affect on organizational performance. J Account Bus Manag 20(1):1–27

Mehran H (1995) Executive compensation structure, ownership, and firm performance. J Financ Econ 38(2):163–184
Oswald SL, Jahera JS Jr (1991) The influence of ownership on performance: an empirical study. Strateg Manag J 12(4):321–326
Otto CA (2014) CEO optimism and incentive compensation. J Financ Econ 114(2):366–404
Pathan S, Faff R (2013) Does board structure in banks really affect their performance? J Bank Financ 37(5):1573–1589
Qiana W, Schaltegger b S (2017) Revisiting carbon disclosure and performance: legitimacy and management views. Br Account Rev 49(4):365–379
Saghi-Zedek N, Tarazi A (2015) Excess control rights, financial crisis and bank profitability and risk. J Bank Financ 55:361–379
Warner JB, Watts RL, Wruck KH (1988) Stock prices and top management changes. J Financ Econ 20:461–492
Whelan T (2021) U.S. corporate boards suffer from inadequate expertise in financially material ESG matters. NYU Stern Center for Sustainable Business. NYU Stern Researchers: Jamie Friedland & Ellen Knuti
Wruck KH (1989) Equity ownership concentration and firm value: evidence from private equity financings. J Financ Econ 23(1):3–28

# Chapter 5
# Corporate Governance and Behavioral Finance

## 5.1 Behavioral Finance and Governance

From the board side, we highlighted the four concepts of bounded rationality, the *problemistic* search, the routinization of decision-making in standard operating procedures, and the political bargaining. From the CEOs' side, we highlighted overconfidence together with present-biased preferences, WACC (weighted average cost capital) fallacy, conservatism bias, and representativeness heuristic.

In this chapter, we describe how a charismatic CEOs ideally can influence fundamental and market performances leveraging on reputation, track record, and confidence. This halo effect can impact major corporate stakeholders as analysts and fund managers leveraging on their behavioral bias. This connection can sometimes transform into a vicious circle bringing to dramatic consequences. We investigated Enron case along with the UK bank scandals in 2008 as examples on how behavioral bias can influence the decision-making process and how this could interrelate with market participants as analysts and fund managers. These examples show how CEOs could successfully capture the most educated among the stakeholders of the market environment creating a toxic environment that generates failures of enormous dimensions.

The relevance of behavioral bias in the decision-making process and their impacts become such a relevant aspect of the organization that some banking supervisors such as DNB,[1] FSA, and APRA[2] decided to include aspects of behavior and culture into their supervisory approach.

A basic principle for that is that ineffective behavior often precedes problems and failures. As such, it seems logical and effective to pay attention to behavior as a financial supervisor. Focusing on behavior would enable supervisors to act in a

[1] Supervision of Behavior and Culture: Foundations, Practice and Future Developments. 2015.
[2] http://www.apra.gov.au/CrossIndustry/Documents/161018-Information-Paper-Risk-Culture.pdf



B. Buchetti, A. Santoni, *Corporate Governance in the Banking Sector*, Contributions to Finance and Accounting, https://doi.org/10.1007/978-3-030-97575-3_5

preemptive manner. Identifying and "intercepting" ineffective behavior at an early stage help to prevent their translation into financial problems.

Financial crisis in the past two decades showed that governance structures were among the root causes of the banking failures. Inadequate boards, unappropriated managerial behavior, CEOs' arrogance and overconfidence, and lack of internal proper culture challenge persistently characterized the most famous bankruptcy cases. Regulators and supervisors in the past two decades put in place significant reforms to banking regulation trying to limit and control the negative consequences of bad governance. However, as former Fed chairman Greenspan said "corporate scandals of recent years have clearly shown that the plethora of laws of the past century have not eliminated the less-savoury side of human behavior."[3]

In this chapter, we will approach the topic of governance structure from a behavioral point of view highlighting the biases present in the board's decision-making process and the CEOs' behaviors.

### *5.1.1 Behavioral Theory and Board*

Behavioral economics looks at how psychology affects economic decision-making. In other words, it looks at how our thoughts, sentiments, and emotions may affect how we make decisions. Behavioral economics explores why we sometimes make irrational decisions. Unlike the field of classical economics, in which decision-making is entirely based on cold-headed logic, behavioral economics allows for irrational behavior and attempts to understand why this may be the case. The concept can be applied to individual situations or more generally to incorporate wider actions of a society or trends in the financial markets.

Behavioral economics after years of hostility by some academics is now a milestone of modern economic discipline. The economics Nobel has already been assigned to a number of researchers who can be classified as behavioral economists, including, Robert Fogel, Daniel Kahneman, Elinor Ostrom, and Robert Shiller. With the addition of Thaler (2017 winner), behavioral economists now account for approximately 6% of all Nobel economics prizes ever awarded.

We believe that the study of governance in banking cannot ignore the behavioral aspect, and we decided to concentrate on the aspects of the governance and limited rationality applied to the decision-making process. From one side, the behavioral theory is related to the board and organization and on the other side the CEO biases.

Conceptualization of organizational decision-making is, according to the most recent literature, built around four concepts: the bounded rationality, the *problemistic* search, the routinization of decision-making in standard operating

[3] https://www.bis.org/review/r040423a.pdf

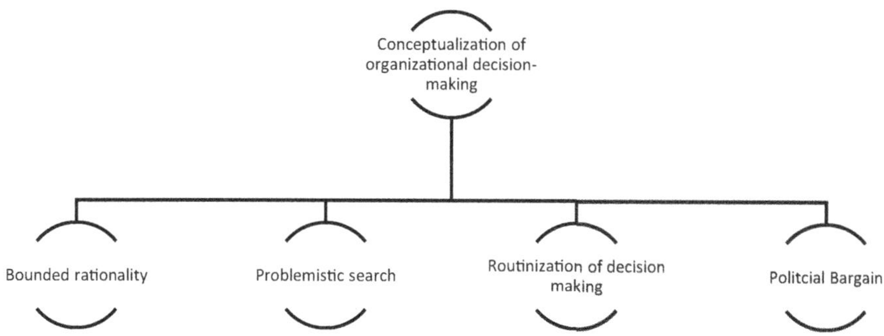


**Fig. 5.1** Behavioral theory and board's decision-making "problematic"

procedures, and the political bargaining (Argote and Greve 2007)[4] as illustrated in Fig. 5.1.

## *5.1.2 Bounded Rationality*

Information overloading, increasing complexity with many alternatives for each scenario, leads to a difficult decision-making process with significant cognitive effort. Bounded rationality suggests that individuals, on the back of these cognitive costs, tend to simplify the decision-making procedure when the problem is complex.[5] Since the decision-making actors do not fully understand the variables involved, they simplify it. This does not necessarily mean that the decision is not utility maximizer. The main consequences are that the decision cannot considered as optimal one but simply it satisfies the specific aspiration level[6] set by social environment, history, or past behavior(s). According to Hendry,[7] limited competence is not always visible to board and CEOs. They may not even recognize the problem themselves, and if they do, their instinct for self-preservation and self-seeking might well tempt them to keep it to themselves.

Sometimes, according to Hendry, these limited competences and unawareness that can be identified as mere opportunism can be real causes of organizational failures and inefficiencies.

---

[4]Argote, L. and Greve, H. R. 2007 A behavioral theory of the firm: 40 years and counting, introduction, and impact, Organization Science, 18: 337–49.

[5]Hans van Ees, Jonas Gabrielsson and Morten Huse. Toward a Behavioral Theory of Boards and Corporate Governance. Corporate Governance: An International Review, 2009, 17(3): 307–319.

[6]Levinthal, D.A. and J.G. March: 1993, "The myopia of learning", Strategic Management Journal 14: 94–112.

[7]Hendry, J.: 2005, "Beyond self-interest: agency theory and the board in a satisficing world", British Journal of Management 16: 55–64.

### 5.1.3 "Problemistic Search"

Cyert and Marchhave theorized the concept of *problemistic search* as the reaction of decision-makers when concerned with immediate problems and short-run solutions. "Problems are only recognized to the extent that an organization has failed to satisfy one or more of its self-imposed goals, or when such failure can be expected in the near future."[8] Because of this attitude, Hendry developed the concept of "satisficing" board's reaction to problem. Basically, given the starting point of *problemistic search*, the reaction would be to accept answers "good enough," short-term solutions to immediate problems.[9] Following this theory, board members are expected to reduce the complexity of decision-making by applying norms, myopic problem-solving heuristics, and memorized routines (see Footnote 5).

Jensen highlights how, among the most important components of board failures, there is its modus operandi and its culture. He points his finger versus the atmosphere of "—... courtesy, politeness and deference at the expense of truth and frankness during board meetings, reflecting a general reluctance of confronting a CEO regarding management decisions, which is seen as both a symptom and cause of failure in the control system."[10]

Bebchuk et al.[11] reinforce this concept citing the corporate culture mantra that overemphasizes concepts such as teamwork, conflict avoidance based on fear of upsetting others, and consensus opinion. These behaviors could be among the root causes to board captured by the chairs or CEOs.

### 5.1.4 Routines

Following the limits of bounded rationality, with the decision-making actors who do not fully understand the variables involved, the satisficing board members are expected to reduce the complexity of decision-making by applying norms and myopic problem-solving heuristics. This process will bring them to memorize routines. Routines can be understood as the learning processes among board members expected to be "operationalized" in the form of procedures and rules for problem-solving, information gathering, and decision-making (see Footnote 5). This operationalization of this process creates decision-making biases.

---

[8] Cyert, R.M. and J.G. March: 1963, A behavioral theory of the firm (Englewoods Cliffs, NJ: Prentice-Hall).

[9] Hendry, J. (2005) Beyond self-interest: Agency theory and the board in a satisficing world, British Journal of Management, 16 (Special issue): 55–64.

[10] Jensen, M.C. (1993). The modern industrial revolution exits and the failure of internal control systems. Journal of Finance. 48, 831–863.

[11] Bebchuk, L.A., Fried, J.M. & Walker, D.I. (2002). Executive compensation in America: Optimal contracting or extraction of rents? The University of Chicago Law Review. Vol. 69, 751–846.

### 5.1.5 *Political Bargaining*

The fourth aspect of the conceptualization of organizational decision-making is represented by the notion of political bargaining or objective setting among coalition of actors. Optimal decision-making process is constrained not only by the limited knowledge, satisficing behavior, and codified memorized routines of the organization but also by board actors organized by coalitions with different objectives and agendas. These possible conflicts are resolved via political bargaining process that could sometimes be conflicts with the best interest of the firms. Suboptimal decision-making process characterized by bias through the whole process could end with political-driven object setting.

The essence of the conceptualization of organizational decision-making from a behavioral point of view is that board actors in their pursue of best interest for the firm are challenged by several biases derived from the dynamics in and around the boardroom.

## 5.2 CEO Biases

CEOs typically report to the board of directors and pursue goals that are meant to drive the company forward, while the board sets those goals. While board is often studied by the literature as a body and group of persons where the decision process dynamics are a key aspect, literature focus more on personal behavior as key attribute for the CEOs. Figure 5.2 illustrates the most common CEOs' biases analyzed.

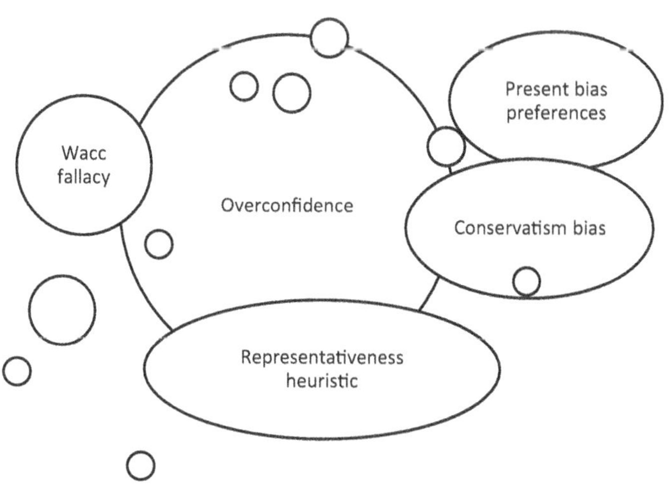


**Fig. 5.2** CEOs' most common biases

### 5.2.1 CEOS' Overconfidence

Research in behavioral finance highlighted that overconfidence is among the most common biases for CEOs in decision-making process. The relevance of the overconfidence bias in practice is confirmed by the fact that 50% of academic paper on managerial biases in the top three finance journals in the period 2000–2016 focus on this bias.[12]

Managers and people in general tend to be optimistic when a decision is made under uncertainty and exhibit overconfidence in judgment (DeBondt and Thaler 1995).[13] This bias tends to influence the perception of overconfident people about their actions, making them appear safer than that of others who exhibit no overconfidence.

Overconfidence plays an important role in situation where uncertainty is highly present as in the stock market. In some uncertain situation, when information is not enough to make rational decision, overconfidence steps in to rationalize a decision.

Among the most common approaches to measuring CEO's overconfidence are approaches toward stock options; managerial forecasts of earnings are also portrayal in the business media to measure CEO's beliefs.

Goel and Thakor (2008)[14] in their paper established a link between overconfidence and the CEO's selection process. They found that an overconfident manager, defined as one who underestimates project risk, has the highest probability of being promoted to CEO when he is competing with otherwise rational managers implying that overconfidence is likely to be a more prevalent attribute among CEOs than in the general population. This is the consequence of the value maximizing selection mechanism that favors overconfident managers who choose higher-risk projects and generate more extreme payoffs.[15] Another reason, underlined by Goel and Thakor (2008), could be that board members are subject to overconfidence biases themselves as such favoring CEOs with similar characteristics. This mechanism has a cascade effect as Malmendier (2018) estimate that overconfident CEOs' probability to appoint an overconfident CFOs is seven times higher than non-overconfident ones (see Footnote 12).

[12]Malmendier, U. (2018). Behavioral Corporate Finance. In D. Bernheim, S. DellaVigna, and D. Laibson (Eds.), Handbook of Behavioral Economics, Volume 1. Elsevier.

[13]DeBondt WFM, Thaler RH: Financial decision-making in markets and firms: a Behavioral perspective. In Handbook in operations research and management science, Vol. 9, Chap. 13. Edited by: Jarrow R, Maksimovic V, Ziemba W. North Holland, Amsterdam: Finance, Elsevier; 1995:385–410.

[14]Goel, A. M. and A. V. Thakor (2008). Overconfidence, CEO selection, and corporate governance. The Journal of Finance 63(6), 2737–2784.

[15]Guenzel, Marius and Malmendier, Ulrike, Behavioral Corporate Finance: The Life Cycle of a CEO Career (August 2020). NBER Working Paper.

Malmendier and Tate (2015)[16] also investigated the potential consequences for corporate in selecting an overconfident CEO. They base their analysis starting from the assumption that CEOs make two main financial investment decisions in a company such as (1) the total level of investment, internal (capital expenditure) and external (M&A), and (2) the split of the financing between internal cash flows and external debt.

Overconfidence would bring CEOs to believe that the market is pricing the equity of the firm too low (underestimating the earning potential of the company) or is pricing the CDS (credit default swap) too high (overestimating the cost of debt). This will bring CEOs to rely more on internal cash flows rather than external financing as new debt or new equity for new investments. On the contrary, the rational CEOs should be neutral on the financing mix choosing the value maximizing level of investment regardless of the split.

One characteristic of overconfident CEOs according to Malmendier and Tate (2015) (see Footnote 16) is that they tend to be more positive to M&A overstating the potential benefits. Deshmukh et al. (2013)[17] analyzed the relation between capital structure and dividend policy with the overconfidence bias of the CEOs. The results show that on average overconfident CEOs tend to determine lower dividend payout policy on the assumption that external financing is costly since not properly priced by the market as such the choice is to retain earnings as much as possible to utilize them for future investments.

In line with their tendency to overestimate their future earnings, overconfident CEOs tend to practice less conservative accounting practices, for example, in delaying recognition of losses[18] leading to nonintentional earnings misstatement. This is also connected to the CEO's willingness to take risky actions. According to prospect theory,[19] individuals undertake risky actions whenever their actual conditions are below their aspirations. Thus, the higher their ambitions, the more individuals are willing to take risks.[20]

Academic literature focuses also on the positive angles of having overconfident CEOs, as the push to innovation. Gervais et al. (2011)[21] found that overconfident managers are more likely be employed in growth firms. The reason is that growth

---

[16] Malmendier, U. and G. Tate (2015). Behavioral CEOs: The Role of Managerial Overconfidence. Journal of Economic Perspectives 29(4), 37–60.

[17] Deshmukh, Sanjay, Anand M. Goel, and Keith M. Howe. 2013. "CEO Overconfidence and Dividend Policy." Journal of Financial Intermediation 22(3): 440–63.

[18] Bouwman, Christa. 2014. "Managerial Optimism and Earnings Smoothing." Journal of Banking and Finance 41(C): 283–303.

[19] Kahneman, D., & Tversky, A. (1979). Prospect theory: An analysis of decision under risk. Econometrica, 47(2), 263–292.

[20] Holmes, R. M, Jr., Bromiley, P., Devers, C. E., Holcomb, T. R., & McGuire, J. B. (2011). Management theory applications of prospect theory: Accomplishments, challenges, and opportunities. Journal of Management, 37(4), 1069–1107.

[21] Gervais, S., J. B. Heaton, and T. Odean (2011). Overconfidence, compensation contracts, and capital budgeting. The Journal of Finance 66(5), 1735–1777.

firms have more upside potential and can offer highly convex compensation schemes. These contracts appeal to overconfident CEOs, who overestimate their ability to create value.

### 5.2.2 *Other CEOS' Biases*

The literature studied some other relevant behavioral biases that have been linked to decision-making process of the CEOs. We will summarize below the most relevant one. One of them is the so-called present-biased preferences. This corresponds to the tendency of people to hyperbolic discounting the future. People's inclination to value the present over the future by more than what exponential discounting would imply whatever they will be doing later will not be as important as what they are doing now.[22] Consequently, this bias will distort investment by investing too early versus the option to wait.

Remaining in the discounting aspect of the investment, another interesting managerial bias demonstrated by research is the WACC fallacy. According to Krüger et al. (2015),[23] firms do not properly adjust for risk in their capital budgeting decisions. This is because managers tend to use a single rate of discount cash flows to value all the different projects of the firms. Consequently, firms will overvalue risky projects at the expense of more stable cash flow projects. Graham and Harvey (2001)[24] in a survey conducted among 392 CFOs revealed that 60% of them use company-wide discount rates to evaluate these projects rather than a project-specific discount rate.

How asset price reacts to new information has been a topic heavily discussed in the behavioral finance literature. Conservatism bias and representativeness heuristic are the related biases. From a managerial point of view, it has been showed that managers tend to systematically underreact to new information sales forecasts consequently delaying adjustments to corporate strategies.[25]

Board's decision-making process and CEOs' biases have been at the center of academic literature studies on behavioral economics following the financial crisis in the first decade of 2000. We described some of the most common irrational beliefs or behaviors that can unconsciously influence board's and CEOs' decision-making process. From the board side, we highlighted four key principles as the *bounded rationality*, the *problemistic* search, the *routinization of decision-making* in standard

[22] Thaler, R. H. and S. Benartzi (2004). Save more tomorrow™: Using Behavioral economics to increase employee saving. Journal of Political Economy 112(S1), S164–S187.

[23] Krüger, P., A. Landier, and D. Thesmar (2015). The WACC fallacy: The real effects of using a unique discount rate. The Journal of Finance 70(3), 1253–1285.

[24] Graham, J. R. and C. R. Harvey (2001). The theory and practice of corporate finance: Evidence from the field. Journal of Financial Economics 60(2–3), 187–243.

[25] Ma, Y., D. A. Sraer, D. Thesmar, and T. Ropele (2020). A Quantitative Analysis of Distortions in Managerial Forecasts. NBER Working Paper No. 26830.

operating procedures, and the *political bargaining*. From the CEOs' side, we highlighted overconfidence together with present-biased preferences, WACC fallacy, conservatism bias, and representativeness heuristic.

## 5.3 Corporate Governance and Stakeholder's Process

We examined the influence of irrational beliefs on the board's and CEOs' decision-making process. The next steps would be to examine how management and CEOs, thanks to charisma and to social influence process, may consciously distort the efficient market hypothesis on price formation. The underlining idea is to investigate the link formed by an unconsciously influenced decision-making process with a consciously distortion. A bad governance could feed himself by exploiting market inefficiencies. We first investigate the literature findings on the link between CEOs' charisma and corporate performances. Secondly, we examine the pervasive influence of a charismatic CEOs toward major corporate stakeholders, as analysts and fund managers, leveraging on their behavioral bias.

### *5.3.1 CEOS' Charisma and Impact on Governance*

The German defined charisma as "a certain quality of an individual personality, by virtue of which s/he is "set apart" from ordinary people and treated as endowed with supernatural, superhuman, or at least specifically exceptional powers or qualities. These as such are not accessible to the ordinary person but are regarded as divine in origin or as exemplary and based on them the individual concerned is treated as a leader."[26]

Today, academic literature defines the power of a charismatic CEOs as the ability to make the organization overcome the major forces that tend to block it from changes.[27] The leader has the skill for inspiring and motivating its employees and stakeholders,[28] the ability to create cohesion between the members of the organization with respect to the mission of the organization.[29] The charisma has a

[26] Dr. David Boje, Charisma lecture notes, Leadership & Society course at New Mexico State University College of Business Administration & Economics, Retrieved 28 July 2005.

[27] Gersick, C.J.G. 1991. Revolutionary change theories: A multilevel exploration of the punctuated equilibrium paradigm. Academy of Management Review, 16: 10–36.

[28] Agle, B.R. 1993. Charismatic chief executive officers: Are they more effective? An empirical test of charismatic leadership theory. Unpublished Doctoral Dissertation. University of Washington. Seattle, WA.

[29] Waldman, D.A. & Yammarino, F.J. 1999. CEO charismatic leadership: Levels-of-management and levels-of-analysis effects. Academy of Management Review, 24:266–285.

fundamental influence in making strategic choices accepted[30] also thanks to the effect a cascade that CEO leadership can have on the entire organization. The ability to predict future trends, and the ability to know how to overcome organizations' inertial forces, represents a clear symptom of charisma for business leaders. The ability to overcoming inertial forces derives from the ability to know how to create attractive visions of the future and promote unconventional solutions to problems.

In an interesting experiment conducted on more than 240 army soldiers, the psychologist Demircan Cakar (2004)[31] demonstrated that there is a high correlation between characteristics typical of perceived leadership (strategic vision, sensitivity to the surrounding environment and staff needs, unconventional behavior) and collective behaviors. These soldiers not only attributed charisma to the person carrying these characteristics, but they standardized their attitudes and their behavior according to the commands of the leader. A charismatic leadership produces collective behaviors that can more easily promote a high standard of employee's performance and quality consequence of the organization.

The level of economic uncertainty, the risks underlying the business, and the objective difficulties organization may represent, according to Hambrick and Finkelstein (1996),[32] are elements which amplify the charisma of a CEO. Cooperation of employees and employee's participation in the project depend on a lot from the leader's ability to exert his/her influence through his/her charisma. In circumstances of uncertainty and crisis, employees certainly need strong directives inclination to accept the influence of the leader may be greater.[33]

Correlation between the charisma of the CEO of an organization and the operational and market performance of the company itself has been at the center of much research. The empirical evidence on the relationship between CEO charisma and organizational performance is mixed.

From one side, Kelly (1967)[34] found evidence that when organizations are perceived of success, this aura of success is then transferred to the CEO. Agle et al. (see Footnote 28) found that CEOs who are perceived to be more charismatic appear to be perceived as more effective concluding that the search for charismatic CEOs may be based more on implicit theory or halo effects than on solid evidence that charisma really does make CEOs more effective.

---

[30] Finkelstein, S. & Hambrick, D.C. 1996. Strategic Leadership: Top executives and their effects. Minneapolis, MN: West Publishing.

[31] Demircan Cakar: The effect of charismatic leadership and collective behaviour on follower performance. July 2004 Cape Town.

[32] Hambrick, D.C. & Finkelstein, 1987. Managerial discretion: A bridge between polar views of organizational outcomes. In L.L. Cummings & B.M. Staw (eds.), Research in Organizational Behaviour (Vol. 9, pp. 369–406). Greenwich, CT: JAI Press.

[33] Shamir, B. & Howell, J.M. 1999. Organizational and contextual influences on the emergence and effectiveness of charismatic leadership. Leadership Quarterly, 10:257–284.

[34] Kelley, H. 1967. Attribution theory in social psychology. Nebraska Symposium on Motivation, 15: 192–240.

On the opposite, Waldman et al. (2001)[35] found no direct relationship between CEO charisma and subsequent organizational performance as measured by net profit margin. Different results are obtained on the effect of the perceived charisma and the stock market performance. Angle et al. (1993) (see Footnote 28) studied a sample of 128 US CEOs with an average lifespan in their role of 6.6 years, an average age of 55, and 770 employees in their respective companies listed. The results showed that there is a strong correlation between charisma perception by the employees and the company's stock market performance.

More consensus among research is found on the benefit of having charismatic CEOs in a crisis scenario or uncertain environment. In a crisis period with greater perceived risk of organizational failure, CEO's discretion may be enhanced, and therefore the influence of their leadership is magnified (see Footnote 32). Charisma and organizational performances can also be negatively correlated. A frequent association between charisma and dysfunctional forms of narcissism could represent a potential downside to charismatic leadership in terms of organizational performance. Sigmund Freud described narcissists as individuals who are emotionally isolated and highly distrustful. Perceived threats can trigger rage. Narcissism can become dangerous for the corporate when, lacking self-knowledge and restraining anchors, he becomes unrealistic dreamer.[36]

## 5.4 Leadership and External Constituents: Analysts and Fund Managers

Many theories and findings suggest examining how the interpersonal influence processes can provide an important source of influence in relationships between management and external constituents as stock analysts and fund managers. We analyze these two stakeholders versus others because they are particularly important for corporates since they influence their stock price and as consequence the possibility, among other things, to raise capital and funding from capital markets.

Stock analysts are paid to write reports on stocks, and on the basis of their quantitative and qualitative conclusions, they determine which stocks deserves a buy or a sell recommendation. A good analyst theoretically can determine the success or failure of a stock on the stock exchange. Analyst is paid to avoid the phenomenon of speculative bubbles and ring the bell in the moment in which the security is considered correctly valued and therefore no longer convenient.

[35] Waldman, D.A., Ramirez, G.A., House, R.J., & Puranam, P. 2001. Does leadership matter? CEO leadership attributes and profitability under conditions of perceived environmental uncertainty. Academy of Management Journal, 44: 134–143.

[36] Maccoby, M. 2000. Narcissistic leaders. Harvard Business Review, 78(1): 68–78.

There is plenty of evidence showing how stock recommendations and earnings forecast revisions can influence stock market valuations.[37] To give the dimension of the relevance of the sector is enough to consider that there are more than 7000 stock equity analysts only in Wall Street.[38] Equity analysts can not only influence institutional investors, but it has been verified that their negative outlook can lead to strategic changes by the company, influence CEOs' compensations, and bring to changes to board members' up to CEOs' resignation.[39]

Stock analysts can influence capital structures of a company by depressing equity valuation as such limiting the possibility of capital increases of possible M&As. CEOs tend to put a lot of attention to stock analysts trying to influence their earnings forecasts and their recommendations by leveraging also on the analysts' behavioral biases.

Overall equity analysts have a lot of power, with the potential capacity to influence the stock market, but at the same time are exposed, as all human beings, to many behavioral biases that can be utilized by corporates at their benefits.

In recent years and with the outbreak of the Internet bubble and the scandals of dot.com, the credibility of financial analysts has taken major hits. Analysts, when they were not considered fraudulent in their recommendations, were at the very least considered in many cases without a critical spirit with a clear attitude of accumulation with respect to the consensus opinion.

Graham (1999)[40] in his study of the behavior of a large sample of US analysts (5293 recommendations of analysts) pointed out that the probability of analysts' herding behavior is inversely related to the following:

1. The analyst's ability, as the awareness of having superior analytical skills, leads the analyst to take an anti-consensus view.
2. The reputational level of the analyst that leads the unknown analyst to making even risky decisions as he/she has nothing to lose with a relationship which is very low risk/reward.
3. The strength of the previous information is as follows: if the consensus is deeply rooted and strengthened from continuous negative judgments by the best-known analysts, then it becomes difficult if not impossible to make the market change its mind even by analysts who are very good.

There is plenty of literature on equity analyst's biases and the potential market dislocations. Welch (2000)[41] has highlighted how the herding behavior from part of

[37] Womack, K. L. 1996. Do brokerage analysts' recommendations have investment value? Journal of Finance, 51: 137–167.

[38] https://www.tipranks.com/

[39] Bhojraj, S., & Sengupta, P. 2003. Effect of corporate governance on bond ratings and yields: The role of institutional investors and outside directors. Journal of Business, 76: 455–475.

[40] Graham J. R., "Herding Among Investment Newsletters: Theory and Evidence", Journal of Finance, 1999, n. 54, pp.237–268.

[41] Welch I., "Herding Among Security Analysts", Journal of Financial Economics, 1999.

the analysts is more evident in the upward phase of the markets and phases characterized by a less information flow. Hurberts (1995)[42] evidenced how the estimates of EPS (earning per share) are statistically too optimistic causing recurring error. Derman and Berry (1995)[43] analyze whether it is useful, for the analyst's reputation, to formulate the "best" estimate. A different prediction from the prevailing one, even if correct in retrospect, is that it can be ex ante more dangerous than rewarding: diversity often in finance does not pay and a forecast close to that of the group, regardless of its accuracy.

Herding behavior protects the analyst's reputation since the mistake made by many is not posteriori attributable to no one in particular. The distortion in analysts' forecasts may therefore be attributable to the fact that the estimates are constructed by seeking consensus, to the detriment of the analyst's professionalism and the fate of its customers. In this hypothesis, the forecasts appear little dispersed with a high average sample value.[44] Cognitive factors such as overconfidence and tendency to ignore disconfirming information are further common biases to which equity analysts are exposed.[45] CEOs may leverage on some of the analyst's biases or peculiarities of their job to obtain a more favorable recommendation.

Westphal and Clement's[46] theory and findings suggest that CEOs exercise social influence processes on equity analysts with the aim to develop and maintain social exchange relations with them. Among the exchanges they indicated are the accesses to critical information and market development that CEOs can guarantee to analysts. CEOs can favor an analyst for corporate road shows or conferences in order to increase analyst's visibility and reputation. CEOs can recommend an analyst for jobs or favor careers. All these elements contribute to build this social exchange reciprocity that may limit analyst's freedom.

Westphal and Bednar (2008)[47] examined 500 US top executives and interviewed 22 top fund managers to investigate how executives may use interpersonal influence behavior to influence also fund managers' behavior and prevent them from using their coercive power to force changes in corporate governance and strategy. Their results support their theory that CEOs would engage in interpersonal influence behavior in the form of ingratiation and persuasion directed at institutional fund

---

[42] Huberts L., Fuller R., "Predictability Bias in the U.S. Equity Market", Financial Analysts Journal, April 1995.

[43] Derman D.N., Berry M.A., "Analyst Forecasting Errors and their Implications for Security Analysis", Financial Analysts Journal, June 1995.

[44] Olsen R.A., "Implications of Herding Behaviour for Earnings Estimation, Risk Assessment, and Stock Returns", Financial Analysts Journal, 1996.

[45] Hong, H., Kubik, J. D., & Solomon, A. 2000. Security analysts' career concerns and herding of earnings forecasts. RAND Journal of Economics, 31: 121–144.

[46] Westphal, J. D., & Clement, M. 2008. Socio-political dynamics in relationships between top managers and security analysts: Favour rendering, reciprocity, and analyst stock recommendations. Academy of Management Journal, 51: 873–897.

[47] Westphal, J. D., & Bednar, M. K. 2008. The pacification of institutional investors. Administrative Science Quarterly, 53: 29–72.

managers reducing the effect of institutional ownership on specific changes in board structure and composition, CEO compensation, and corporate strategy that are believed to compromise management's interests.

Scharfestein and Stein (1990)[48] propose an analysis to study behavior in choices of investment by managers of large mutual funds or hedge funds. They demonstrated that fund managers are not immune from herd behavioral bias. Their results showed that fund managers are on average unsure about their stock picking ability and tend to conform to other professional investors. This allows him to hide his lack of skill behind a group error, not attributable to anyone. This attitude rewards the manager uncertain in his/her choices, and if other managers are in a similar situation, then an aggregate imitation phenomenon occurs between major investors.

A charismatic CEO ideally can influence fundamental and market performances leveraging on reputation, track record, and confidence. This halo effect can impact major corporate stakeholders as analysts and fund managers leveraging on their behavioral bias. This connection can sometimes transform into a vicious circle bringing to dramatic consequences.

## 5.5 Management Bias and Market Inefficiencies

We analyzed how behavioral bias can influence the decision-making process and how this could interrelate with market participants as analysts and fund managers incentivizing CEOs to social exchange process that could create a potential toxic environment. In this paragraph, we see some concrete cases of how this phenomenon materialized.

### *5.5.1 The Case of Enron*

Enron was formed in 1985 in Texas through the merger of two gas companies, Houston Natural Gas and InterNorth. Its chairman and CEO managed to bring Enron in the Olympus of the top 500 US companies. By early 2001, Enron had evolved to the largest buyer/seller of natural gas and electricity with revenues reaching more than $10 billion becoming the seventh largest corporation in the world, based upon revenues. Following a series of accounting scandals, however, Enron's stock price started to drop from $90.75 in August 2000 to $0.26 by closing on November 30, 2001, with a loss of $70 billion for its shareholders.

The slide of the share value was slow but persistent during the all period from August 2000 to the bankruptcy. It was prompted by rumors on the quality of Enron's

[48] Scharfestein D., Stein J., "Herd Behaviour and Investment", American Economic Review, n.80, 1990.

earnings and its balance sheet strength. This was in conjunction with significant insider stock sales by senior executives. Corporate governance's issues exacerbated the situation with the resignation of Enron's chief executive officer in August 2001, while in October 2001, Enron reported $618 million quarterly loss. In the meantime, the US Securities and Exchange Commission (SEC) was launched investigating on potential conflicts of interests. This ended with Enron's management admitting, in November 2001, that profits had been overstated by $600 million since 1997 forcing the company to restate the full balance sheet.

Finally, at the end of November 2001, Enron filed for bankruptcy protection in New York, and in May of 2002, Neal Batson was appointed to serve as the examiner for the Enron Corp. The examiner concluded that "Enron manipulated its financial statements in violation of GAAP and failed to make appropriate disclosures to the public of its SPE transactions under applicable disclosure standards."[49]

We will not focus for this case on the techniques utilized by Enron to hide losses or to upfront future cash flows to overstate earnings. Rather we will focus on CEOs' behavior toward the market.

### 5.5.2 *Analysts*

Given the valuation methodologies utilized by equity analysts (based on price earnings valuation or discount cash flows), Enron's overstated earnings would impact positively valuation and consequently market capitalization. It does no surprise that as of October 18,[50] all 15 analysts tracked by the Thomson Financial/ First Call rated Enron a "buy" or "strong buy." What it is surprising is that few days after Enron disclosed the accounting issues related to the past 5 years, 11 of the 15 analysts were still recommending buying the stock. One of the most important Wall Street analysts wrote in his report[51] (recommending the stock as a strong buy) the following:

- "We do not intend to completely dismiss investor concerns or all of the negative stories that are circulating about Enron. Some appear to have validity. However, most appear to represent major exaggeration or misinformation, and even these are difficult to effectively debunk given Enron's limited financial disclosure."
- "Investors have begun to call Enron's earnings a "black box" as they began to doubt their ability to analyze and predict future earnings.... Enron management is now committed to improving disclosure, even at the expense of competitive issues."

---

[49] https://www.justice.gov/archive/ust/press/docs/pr_enron_examiner052202.htm

[50] https://www.forbes.com/2002/02/27/0227analysts.html?sh=b42d9ec14354

[51] https://www.justice.gov/archive/enron/exhibit/02-21/BBC-0001/Images/EXH062-00068.PDF, https://www.ft.com/content/80a6ee52-98ee-4ccc-8183-a68968c5fc9a, https://www.crottaz-finance.ch/blog/wp-content/uploads/2013/06/GS-reco-Enron-9-10-01.pdf

- "Many top managers have left, leaving a vacuum at the senior levels of Enron. Insiders have been heavy sellers of Enron shares...... However, in each case, an extremely capable successor has stepped in to fill the hole" (see Footnote 51).

It is surprising the amount of contradiction in few sentences between his recommendation (strong buy) and a logic guided by common sense.

Four Wall Street analysts testifying at the trail said they felt no pressure either from Enron's management or their own firms to manipulate earning expectation to support the stock. Rather, they all believed, based on public information and their own analyses, that Enron's "core business" was profitable and sound as its business model. These considerations would sound plausible and sensible before November 8, and the admission by Enron of accounting manipulation, but they appear difficult to sustain after it. We believe that the analysts' bias and the CEOs' social influence may explain a significant part of the analyst's behavior in the Enron's case. Empirical evidence shows that due to behavioral biases, analyst tend to do the following:

- Analysts do not promptly identify new information connected to earnings surprises.
- Analysts behave overconfidently with respect to their prior views.
- Analyst's underweight signals disconfirm their prior views while overweight confirming signs.
- Analysts tend to classify a permanent change as a temporary one when useful to confirm his view.

Some of the analysts utilized reported Enron's accounting information without questioning the reliability of such data itself. This is notwithstanding; they publicly and widely acknowledged the fact that Enron lacked transparent accounting practices.

Munawer (2012)[52] examined how sell-side security analysts processed Enron's misleading financial statements during the period 1997–2001. The major result was that analysts utilized reported accounting information issued by Enron without questioning the reliability of such data itself. This is notwithstanding; analysts publicly and widely acknowledged the fact that Enron lacked transparent accounting practices. Contrary to their role, analysts build their analysis on accounting numbers issued by Enron, a company with weak transparency, without questioning or examining the numbers themselves. Analysts seemed to have been captured by CEOs' charisma and company's reputation, while their herding behaviors prevent them to react rationally to new information. A clear example was the analyst's reaction to the Enron CEOs' resignation on August 14, 2001. The company announced that the resignation was due to personal reasons and analysts repeated this justification in their reports with no change in recommendation or significant change in estimates. CEOs apparently managed to capture also the staff considering that while he was selling a large amount of his Enron's stocks, he encouraged Enron's employees to

[52]Munawer, Yahya, Nabiha: Sell-side Security Analysts: Re-reporting of Enron Corporation Fraudulent Financial Data October 2012 Procedia - Social and Behavioral Sciences 62:749–760.

buy more shares. While he was assuring equity analysts on the quality of earning, he guaranteed the staff that the company was on the rebound.

In banking, the relation between equity analysts and UK and Irish banking system from 2000 up to 2010 can be considered another case of heuristic applied to investment decision process. In an interview to the UK press, *The Guardian*,[53] an equity analyst described this form of reverence as follows:

> The cult surrounding Fred Goodwin[54] is an example of capture. Around Northern Rock. Around the Irish banks, even more. A lot of analysts will admit in retrospect that somewhere in their minds they knew things were dodgy all along. But everyone bought into the myth. Remember, for 4, 5 years these banks produced only good news. It takes some balls to call up 50 guys every morning and tell them the entire stock market is wrong.

Kahneman and Tversky (1979)[55] have demonstrated that investors have not always used a rational approach in dealing with the decisions of investment. The psychologist Solomon Asch (1952)[56] with an experiment tried to demonstrate the great power of the social influence on individual judgment. The scientist applied an approach constructive to social influence, and through famous experiments, he demonstrated the influence of a majority on perception. In 1956, he organized an experiment in which he called eight people, seven of whom are accomplices, to draw five lines in descending order, naming A the first and B the second on a blackboard, and then asked people to point to the longest line. Obviously, the accomplices always answer B, and he records that in 90% of cases; also the eighth people responded like other people. The individual perceives others and their opinion as indispensable points of reference, not irrational sources of stimulus but organs constituting the cognitive field. A different interpretation of the experiment was given by the psychologists Deutsch and Gerard (1955)[57] who tended to consider the attitude of the individual not as an adaptation to the masses but as a belief that it was impossible for such a large group of people to commit mistake. Guided by this conviction, they adapted by succumbing to the law of the great numbers.

Enron case along with the UK banks is an example on how behavioral bias can influence the decision making process and how this could interrelate with market participants as analysts and fund managers. These examples show how CEOs could successfully capture the most educated among the stakeholders of the market

[53] https://www.hitc.com/en-gb/2012/06/14/banking-equity-analyst-at-major-bank-some-days-its-the-best-job/

[54] Chief Executive Officer (CEO) of the Royal Bank of Scotland Group (RBS) between 2001 and 2009.

[55] Kahnemann D., Tversky A. (1979) "Prospect Theory: An analysis of decision under risk", Econometrica and Kahnemann D., Tversky A. (1984) "Choices, values and frames", American Psychologist.

[56] Solomon A., "Social Psychology", Englewood Cliffs, N.J.: Prentice Hall, 1952. Trad. It. "Psicologia Sociale", Torino, SEI, 1989.

[57] Deutsch M., Gerard H.B., "A Study of Normative and Informational Social Influences upon Individual Judgement", Journal of Abnormal and Social Psychology, n.51, 1955, pp. 629–636.

environment creating a toxic environment that generates failures of enormous dimensions.

## 5.6 Behavioral Economics and Supervision

The relevance of behavioral bias in the decision-making process becomes such a relevant aspect of the organization that some banking supervisors such as DNB,[58] FSA, and APRA[59] decided to include aspects of behavior and culture into their supervisory approach.

A basic principle for that is that ineffective behavior often precedes problems and failures. As such, it seems logical and effective to pay attention to behavior as financial supervisor. Focusing on behavior would enable supervisors to act in a preemptive manner. Identifying and "intercepting" ineffective behavior at an early stage help to prevent their translation into financial problems.

### *5.6.1 Behavioral Economics and Banking Supervision*

According to the Deloitte's Global Human Capital Trends Report (2020), only 12% of executives surveyed around the world rate considered direction from their boards and leaders as major drivers of the increasing importance of ethics in the future of work, versus 38% considered legal and regulatory requirements as the key driver. Similar shocking results were highlighted in the Deloitte's Global Human Capital Trends Report (2016) where 86% of executives surveyed rated culture as "very important" or "important" but only 12% of companies believe their organizations were driving the "right culture." It seemed that there is awareness about a potential cultural issue but lacks an internal push for a change.

Dutch Central Bank in 2010, following the 2008 financial crisis, decided to increase its attention on the behavioral side of governance having a predictive quality indicator from a prudential point of view (see Footnote 58). DNB tested different methodologies for supervising behavior and culture of financial institutions.

In their supervision activity, the central bank set criteria to identify the risks associated with the leadership role of CEOs/top management or board members. The criteria are divided in three blocks as personal level (vision), interaction level (influence), and organizational level (dependency).

On the personal level, the indicators monitored are the following:

[58] https://www.dnb.nl/media/1gmkp1vk/supervision-of-behaviour-and-culture_tcm46-380398-1.pdf

[59] http://www.apra.gov.au/CrossIndustry/Documents/161018-Information-Paper-Risk-Culture.pdf

**Purpose.** Supervisors check if the leader has created a goal and a vision in the company. Employees should know the end goal of the company and should be aware of the vision of his leader. Leader should have among his skills the capacity to self-reflect on his performance and apply lesson learned process. Within the personal level skills, CEO should show an adaptive leadership, meaning the capacity to continuously develop and adjust his/her behavior according to the different circumstances, for example, to accept staff's suggestions and make his/her leadership role as participative as possible in normal times to capture bottom-up proposals. During crisis times, this behavior should adapt to the times with more centralization and directive style.

DNB during the past few years exercised several investigations among major local financial institutions and reported that they have identified several governance deficiencies. The most common one is the attention of CEO to the technical aspects of his/her staff rather than behavioral and human aspects. CEOs oversimplify the potential behavioral impact of determined company choices. CEOs lacked awareness of the complexity of behavioral changes. This, according to DNB, decreases the leadership effect.

CEOs often demonstrated lack of time to proceed to a serious self-reflection of their behavior. This is reflected in several interviews conducted by DNB.

The second level investigated by the supervisors during their inspections to the financial institutions is the interaction level associated with the capacity of the leader to influence others to reach determined goals for the financial institutions. This influence should be performed in a convincing way and with a certain level of humility by the CEOs. DNB is aware that overconfidence is among the most common biases of human being and leaders.

This power to influence is based on certain CEOs' characteristics such as charisma, legitimacy, know-how, and reputation, among others. CEOs need to create the conditions to spread this influence. DNB, in his supervisory methodology, makes very concrete examples. One of this is room for discussions where staff has the possibility to freely interact among them to discuss about ideas and risks associated with the business. In their inspections, DNB checks if leaders create the opportunities to speak freely and invite them to do so. Leaders are expected to push staff out of the comfort zone without stressing them to accelerate the career development and the formation.

The process of interaction level develops on goal setting. These should be set by leaders in a realistic way. Leaders are expected to know and understand the power of setting realistic and effective targets within the firm.

The third level is about the organizational level and the dependency level.

DNB examines two dependencies of CEO factors: internal and external. With internal dependency, they identify the leadership role of the CEOs toward the employees. Internal respect is gained and valued by reputation, leadership charisma, and performances. Supervisors in their investigation activity monitor if leader is aware of this role modeling inside the organization. In this sense, ethical leadership is among the first aspects examined considering the idiosyncratic importance of this aspect and the ramification impact that an unethical leadership could have inside the organization and outside it. Congruence between intention and actual behavior in everyday life is among other aspects as object of investigation.

External dependency is toward the other stakeholders that range from shareholders, customers, supervisors, regulators, and other authorities. The role of the CEOs is to maximize the positive feedback coming from his leadership relationship with these stakeholders. The overall expectation of the Dutch supervisors is that financial institutions' management is aware of these dependencies, and they carefully manage them in their daily activity. The marketing and external activity should be transparent, honest, and aligned with stakeholders' interest and perceptions.

### 5.6.2 Group Dynamics

One of the aspects considered with attention by DNB is the group dynamics within the top management team in a financial firm. This could be an important red flag for supervisors potentially showing behavioral risks. With group dynamics, DNB defines "the interaction between different positions and patterns within a group or between groups, which affect overall group effectiveness" (see Footnote 58). Within the group dynamics, DNB assesses the composition and the dynamics. For the composition, DNB evaluates with attention diversity and size. An appropriate mix of expertise and know-how is well regarded. In terms of size, an optimal size is the one that is big enough to allow diversity and small enough to avoid dispersion of diversity and point of views. Among other things, supervisor's expectations incorporate attention, by board and CEOs, to talent development and succession planning.

Supervisors during the onsite inspection of a financial group assess the group climate by exploring four different dimensions: (a) the nature of interpersonal relationships, (b) the degree of cohesiveness in a group, (c) the way the group deals with conflicts, and (d) the balance between task and relationship orientation within a group.

Constructive relations between group members are symptoms of a good climate. A defensive interpersonal relationship often characterized a blaming climate and lack of good communication.

Degree of cohesiveness is the tendency for a group to work unitedly for reaching the firm's goal. Too much cohesiveness could bring to behavioral bias as group conformity. The capacity of the group to deal with dissenting opinion is an important element for judging a good cohesiveness by DNB.

The way the group deals with conflicts is the third element considered to judge a group climate. A group able to have open discussion in active manner is a good indicator of positive climate.

The last element taken in consideration is the connection between duty and relationship orientation as contributor to the effectiveness of a group dynamics.

Supervisors expect that board and CEOs pay attention to these aspects and put in place remedial actions in case some of these features are not tackled adequately.

### 5.6.3 Error Management

Another interesting aspect studied by DNB is the error management within the financial institution. In the past financial crisis, the usual initial reactions by banks toward scandals, mistakes, and operational losses were to blame the staff involved to punish the culprits and to give a signal to the other stakeholders that it was only their responsibility. Further to this, banks and regulators usually have implemented additional criteria and rules to prevent future mistakes. In parallel, banks tended to reinforce line of defenses to strengthen the control functions. However, history tells that this strategy was not able to prevent mistakes to repeat again and again even in the same financial institution.

DNB developed an additional strategy to limit the reiteration of mistakes. DNB focused on the cultural and behavioral aspect of the error management. Error should not be treated with blame and penalized. This attitude could bring to several unwanted consequences as tentative of the individual to not speak up about the mistake or even worst to cover it. Error should instead be treated as a normal part of the company life and accepted as an inevitable. This would create an atmosphere of open dialogue inside the firm. This dialogue would be fundamental to face timely mistakes and spread a culture of learning process from past errors. The ideal environment suggested by DNB is an organizational approach to error that is tolerant but with a proactive response.

On the opposite, firms should avoid denial, blame, and punishment or empathy (tolerance but passive approach). In practice, financial companies are expected to implement a communicating reporting procedure and establish internal point of contacts to report mistakes. Meetings should be organized to speak openly about past mistakes and lessons learned and measures put in place to avoid them. Companies should develop internal facilitators that encourage open dialogue during these meetings.

Leaders and CEOs should create a learning culture climate and open communication toward errors.

### 5.6.4 DNB Behavioral and Culture Inspection Types

DNB published in the *Supervision of Behavior and Culture* (see Footnote 58) has inspection approach and objective related to typical behavioral and culture inspection types. It identified four inspection types related to board effectiveness, change effectiveness, risk culture, and root cause analysis.

The Dutch supervisor in checking board effectiveness and the other topics uses an approach based on onsite inspection. The inspection objective is to get "insight into risks related to a board's decision-making, leadership, communication, and group dynamics which impair effective board performance" (see Footnote 58).

On change effectiveness, the focus would be on "strengths and weaknesses in terms of translating the vision, willingness to change, implementation, and ability to learn."

Among the most important focus regarding the risk culture of onsite team would be to assess if there would be "behavioral patterns that could have a detrimental impact on decisions on risk awareness, risk taking, and risk management."

Lastly DNB's onsite inspector will try to investigate if the bank has "developed an effective mitigation strategy that intervenes in the drives of the unsound and ineffective behavioral patterns " (see Footnote 58).

## 5.7 Conclusion

Banking scandals and several years of supervision experience convinced the Dutch banking supervisor DNB, among others, to integrate behavioral and corporate culture into the area of risk investigation to prevent crisis. Group dynamics within the board, culture change, countervailing powers, CEOs' leadership, and error management are among the most prominent problems highlighted by supervisory report addressed to banks. Supervision is not only a matter of risk identification from a quantitative point of view as it could be credit or market risk but rather start from the analysis of the governance structure and corporate culture.

## References

Argote L, Greve HR (2007) A behavioral theory of the firm: 40 years and counting, introduction, and impact. Organ Sci 18:337–349

Cakar D (2004) The effect of charismatic leadership and collective behaviour on follower performance. Cape Town

DeBondt WFM, Thaler RH (1995) Financial decision-making in markets and firms: a behavioral perspective, Chap. 13. In: Jarrow R, Maksimovic V, Ziemba W (eds) Handbook in operations research and management science, vol 9. Elsevier, North Holland, pp 385–410

Deshmukh S, Goel AM, Howe KM (2013) CEO overconfidence and dividend policy. J Financ Intermed 22(3):440–463

Gervais S, Heaton JB, Odean T (2011) Overconfidence, compensation contracts, and capital budgeting. J Financ 66(5):1735–1777

Goel AM, Thakor AV (2008) Overconfidence, CEO selection, and corporate governance. J Financ 63(6):2737–2784

Graham JR, Harvey CR (2001) The theory and practice of corporate finance: evidence from the field. J Financ Econ 60(2–3):187–243

Kahneman D, Tversky A (1979) Prospect theory: an analysis of decision under risk. Econometrica 47(2):263–292

Kelley H (1967) Attribution theory in social psychology. Neb Symp Motiv 15:192–240

Krüger P, Landier A, Thesmar D (2015) The WACC fallacy: the real effects of using a unique discount rate. J Financ 70(3):1253–1285

Malmendier U (2018) Behavioral corporate finance. In: Bernheim D, DellaVigna S, Laibson D (eds) Handbook of behavioral economics, vol 1. Elsevier, Amsterdam
Malmendier U, Tate G (2015) Behavioral CEOs: the role of managerial overconfidence. J Econ Perspect 29(4):37–60
Munawer Y (2012) Nabiha: sell-side security analysts: re-reporting of Enron corporation fraudulent financial data. Procedia Soc Behav Sci 62:749–760
Scharfestein D, Stein J (1990) Herd behaviour and investment. Am Econ Rev 80(3):465–479
Waldman DA, Ramirez GA, House RJ, Puranam P (2001) Does leadership matter? CEO leadership attributes and profitability under conditions of perceived environmental uncertainty. Acad Manag J 44:134–143
Welch I (2000) Herding among security analysts. J Financ Econ 58(3):369–396

# Chapter 6
# Why Corporate Governance Matters: Spectacular Defaults

In the following chapter, we concentrate our attention to specific banking crisis events to pass from the theory to the practice and identify concrete governance failure cases. Grant Kirkpatrick of OECD (Economic Co-operation and Development) (2009)[1] analyzed, in his corporate governance lessons from the financial crisis, the relationship between weak corporate governance and failures on several banking crises highlighting the strong correlation. He underlined that the 2006–2008 financial meltdown was characterized by severe shortcomings in internal governance, in risk management, and in the role of the board in overseeing risk management. These failures ranged from the following:

- Lack of understanding by the board of the inherent risks of the instruments carried in the balance sheet.
- Lack of knowledge by the board's risk appetite limits and control mechanisms, both typically a topical board's responsibility.
- Risk management information was not always provided properly and timely to the board.
- Due to a silo approach to risk management, the sharing of risk information was ineffective.
- Deficiencies in the capacity to read results contained in forward-looking stress test scenario and/or to design the proper scenarios.

The original version of this chapter was revised: chapter title and text corrections updated. The correction to this book can be found at https://doi.org/10.1007/978-3-030-97575-3_7

Disclaimer: this chapter is based only on publicly available sources. For each case we use fictitious names to protect companies' and peoples' confidentiality.

[1]Grant Kirkpatrick: The Corporate Governance Lessons from the Financial Crisis. ISSN 1995–2864 Financial Market Trends OECD 2009.



B. Buchetti, A. Santoni, *Corporate Governance in the Banking Sector*, Contributions to Finance and Accounting, https://doi.org/10.1007/978-3-030-97575-3_6

- In some banks, the difference in perceived status of risk management staff vis-à-vis traders determined failure to properly and timely escalate red flags to the appropriate level in the organization.
- Distorted remuneration policies and incentive systems created harmful conditions incentivizing unsustainable balance sheet positions.

In the following paragraphs, we described the main governance issues in different spectacular banking bankruptcy events (pre- and post-2008 financial crisis). We decided to select specific cases as in Lehman Brothers, BCCI (Bank of Credit and Commerce International), Herstatt Bank, Societe Generale, and UBS since they summarize from different angles most of the different governance loopholes that could create the conditions for a banking failure.

## 6.1 Lehman Brothers

One of the most interesting reading on the spectacular default of Lehman Brothers is the examiner's report released to the public in March 2010.[2]

On September 15, 2008, at 1:45 A.M., Lehman Brothers filed for the largest bankruptcy proceeding ever something that nearly caused a meltdown of the world's financial system. Lehman's bankruptcy was analyzed and explained with several technical reasons mainly focusing on excessive leverage and excessive credit risk, among others. It is undisputable however that the trigger that dragged Lehman into bankruptcy was its inability to retain the confidence of its lenders and counterparties and as consequence it run short of liquidity. In this chapter, we analyze the governance aspect of this spectacular default. Among the most relevant corporate issues highlighted by the Valukas' reports, there is "failure of government oversight, bad management decision, errors in business judgement till deliberate balance sheet manipulation."

Here we would like to highlight some of the most relevant technical reasons while focusing in the second part on the analysis of the governance root causes.

Leverage (excessive) was one of the key aspects of the Lehman's business model at the time. The balance sheet of Lehman Brothers augmented from $312 billion at the end of 2003 to $786 billion in the first quarter (2008) with an increase of 152%. Equity during the same period increased from $13 billion to $24 billion with the gross leverage (asset/equity) increasing from around 23 times to 32 times. The issue was that when banks operate with such highly leverage, small changes in assumptions about the value of their assets can have massive implications for the valuation of their equity.

Asset opacity, or the difficulty to assign a reliable price to an asset, was another characteristic of the Lehman's balance sheet. According to the International Financial Reporting Standards,[3] assets calculated at fair value (vast majority for an

[2]Lehman Brothers Holdings Inc. Chapter 11 Proceedings Examiner's Report. https://web.stanford.edu/~jbulow/Lehmandocs/menu.html.

[3]https://www.ifrs.org/

investment bank) can be categorized into three levels depending on the inputs used in valuation techniques. In particular, these are the following:

- Level 1 assets when inputs are traded prices in active markets.
- Level 2 assets when inputs are observable for most of the terms of the asset.
- Level 3 assets when inputs are unobservable including information derived through extrapolation or interpolation of observable market data.

It goes without saying that Level 3 assets valuation is opaque and could lead to several overvaluation, potentially hiding losses. According to Lehman's financial data, at the end of second quarter (2007), the total amount of Level 3 assets represented 104% of the equity of the bank. At the end of the first quarter (2008), this amount increased to 170% with 60% of Level 3 assets represented by mortgages. The issue was that investors become very skeptical about the real valuation of the bank's equity. Moreover, the high volume of illiquid assets made it much more difficult for the firm to raise equity or funding, to hedge risks, or to sell assets to reduce the leverage in its balance sheet.

Liquidity, or better lack of liquidity, was the fundamental reason of the Lehman's bankruptcy. Banks' funding comes from a mixture of debt and equity. The debt, in turn, can be divided into secured and unsecured funding and long and short terms. In the case of Lehman, most of the funding was via repo for an economical reason. It would have been uneconomical for Lehman, with such leverage, to raise hundreds of billions in commercial paper markets. In the case of repo, the counterparty receives securities as collateral for the life of the transaction as a protection in the event of the borrower defaulting. This allowed Lehman to raise funding cheaper at high volumes. At the end of 2007, Lehman reported that less than 35% of its funding was long term versus 50% funding represented by repos. Few months before the bankruptcy (May 2008), 46% of the own financial instruments were pledged to raise funding for a total of $269 billion. In normal times, this number could potentially not represent a significant warning element given the large and liquid repo market. In a crisis when the bank borrowing appears to be in trouble, then lenders are often forced to pull back. The withdrawal might materialize in different ways as an increase in haircuts, a reduction in maturity, a refusal to repo more illiquid types of collateral, or a termination of trading with a given counterparty. The issue is that, considering that the average maturity of Lehman repos was around 40 days,[4] if Lehman would, as it did, lose access to the repo market due to loss in trust by the counterparties, in about 1 month, it would lose half of its funding, going bust.

### 6.1.1 Corporate Governance Issues

Examiner's report highlighted that a bad corporate governance exacerbated the Lehman's financial difficulties and the consequences to Lehman's creditors and

[4]Lehman 10-Qs. Typically excludes repo of government bonds and agencies.

shareholders. Lehman's executives' conduct ranged "from serious but non-culpable errors of business judgment to actionable balance sheet manipulation." Examiner highlighted few methods utilized by Lehman's management to manipulate market perception on the real status of the balance sheet of the bank.

One of the most important balance sheet manipulations utilized from the management was the so-called Repo 105. This accounting trick was particularly useful to shed some positive light on the restructuring process to rating agencies and equity analysts particularly keen to see a downward trend on the net leverage. Examiner (2010) described how Repo 105 worked: "Normal repo transactions consisted of selling assets with the obligation of repurchase within a few days. Considered a financing event, these "sold" items stayed on the bank's balance sheet. Repo 105 made use of an accounting rule where, if the assets sold were valued at more than 105% of cash received, the transaction could be called a true sale and the assets removed from Lehman's books. $50 billion of assets were removed from the balance sheet in this way, improving their leverage ratio from 13.9 to 12.1 at the time.... Lehman did not disclose its use – or the significant magnitude of its use – of Repo 105 to the Government, to the rating agencies, to its investors, or to its own Board.... Lehman's auditors were aware of but did not question Lehman's use and nondisclosure of the Repo 105 accounting transactions."[5]

Another likely market manipulation highlighted by the examiner is the misleading information regarding the liquidity pool available to Lehman to face the crisis. According to the official documentation throughout 2008, Lehman had available $40 billion of liquidity pool. Unfortunately, Lehman did not disclose the fact that by June 2008, significant components of its reported liquidity pool had become difficult to monetize and that a substantial part of the pool was in fact encumbered or illiquid.

Lehman's risk management personnel suggest that Lehman's senior management disregarded its risk managers, its risk policies, and its risk limits. Examiner (2010) reports several internal emails to prove this attitude. An email from two senior risk managers highlighted "....... whatever risk governance process we had in place was ultimately not effective in protecting the firm [.] Risk Appetite measures were not effective in establishing clear enough warning signals that the Firm was taking on too much risk relative to capital. . .. The [Risk Management] function lacked sufficient authority within the Firm. Decision-making was dominated by the business. . .."); e-mail from other very senior managers .... "I am shocked at the poor risk mgmt. at the highest levels, and I don't think it started with Archstone. It is all unbelievable and I think there needs to be an investigation into the broader issue of malfeasance. Mgmt. gambled recklessly with thousands of jobs and shareholder wealth...."

Lehman's management failed to update one of the most important tools for risk control, the stress test. In the May 2008 stress test delivered to the SEC, Lehman did not properly account for the market reaction in a stressed liquidity event and did not

[5] Examiner's Interview of Ernst & Young, Repo 105 session, Oct. 16, 2009, at pp. 8–9 (statement of William Schlich); Examiner's Interview of Ernst & Young, Nov. 3, 2009, at pp. 14–15 (statement of Hillary Hansen).

revise its stress testing to address its evolving new deteriorated conditions and a different business strategy.

Under the same line, Lehman had a series of "risk appetite limits" designed to discipline the risk framework. One of the issues was the pro-cyclical approach to this management. In 2007, when the signs of macro deterioration were emerging management decided to increase these limits to justify it, Lehman apparently changed the way that it calculated the limits. Examiner reported that "in late 2007 and early 2008, Lehman relaxed its risk appetite limits in several other ways… as an example Lehman did not apply the single transaction limit to its commercial real estate deals. In sum, during the second half of 2006, Lehman began to pursue a more aggressive principal investment strategy, and it relaxed several risk limits to facilitate that strategy."

Communication between management and the board was not always linear and candid. Examiner in his report recalled a presentation in March 2007 where the Mortgage Division presented to the board the state of Lehman's residential mortgage portfolio following clear signs of stress in the sector. The Mortgage Division "emphasized that Lehman's management considered the crisis an opportunity to pursue a countercyclical strategy."

An email published by the examiner between managers preparing the material for the meeting mentioned the following:

> *Board is not sophisticated around subprime market – Joe doesn't want too much detail. He wants to candidly talk about the risks to Lehman but be optimistic and constructive – talk about the opportunities that this market creates and how we are uniquely positioned to take advantage of them.*[6]

The information provided to the board and the market about the real liquidity position of the bank were rather optimistic. Lehman's global treasurer reported to the board's finance and risk committee that Lehman had record levels of liquidity and cash capital surplus at the end of the third quarter of 2007. He declared that "liquidity pool year-to-date and over the last 4 years, noting the conservative nature of the firm's liquidity pool as compared to its peers, which [had] been recognized by the leading credit rating agencies."[7] Examiner reports that "Management did not tell the Board or the Finance and Risk Committee about ALCO's concerns about Lehman's ability to fund its commitments, or that Lehman had nearly stopped entering into new deals in August 2007."[8]

An interesting aspect underlined by the examiner is the overload of information available to the management that provide an appeal on some selected disclosure provided to the board. Examiner reported that "although Lehman's management did not provide the Board with all available information concerning the risks faced by the firm during 2007 and early 2008, that fact is not surprising given the Board's

---

[6]E-mail from Examiner's report.

[7]Lehman Brothers Holdings Inc., Minutes of Meeting of Finance and Risk Committee of the Board of Directors (Sept. 11, 2007), at p. 3 [LBEX-AM 067018].

[8]Examiner's Interview June 25, 2009, at pp. 16–17.

limited role in overseeing the firm's risk management, and the extraordinarily detailed information available to management."

Moreover, according to the examiner, the information available to the management as risk limits, policies, and metrics were designed for use by management, not the board.

Several other corporate governance issues were impacting the business as a significant executive turnover or countercyclical business strategy predicated from the management to the board also via biased information that depicted the mortgages price weakness an opportunity to take market share and as consequence the late awareness of the dimension of the crisis and the late sell of distressed assets.

The compensation scheme according to the examiner was designed to penalize excessive risk-taking. On paper, staff were rewarded via a "compensation scorecard" that included risk-weighted metrics such as return on equity (ROE) and return on asset (ROA), value at risk (VAR), and risk appetite. In practice, Lehman compensation scheme was based simply on revenue with minimal attention to risk factors underlying them, with minimal or absent risk-related adjustment factors applied.

Examiner reports that "to calculate revenue for its compensation pool, Lehman included revenue not yet recognized but recorded based on mark-to-market positions. In theory, therefore, traders and business units were incentivized to enter transactions for short-term profits, even if those transactions created long-term risks for the firm."

The Lehman Brothers' bankruptcy examiner, at the end of his report, highlighted that the decisions by Lehman's management (and as we mentioned the mistakes that followed these decisions) must also be considered in context. He did not find enough evidence of gross negligence to establish that a duty of care was breached. Examiner concluded that Delaware Law, which governed Lehman as a Delaware corporation, allowed Lehman's officers to pursue this aggressive high-risk strategy. The examiner could not question their business decision to do so since they considered to be at the *core of the business judgment role*. At the same time, the examiner did find that Lehman's management voluntary opted for disregarding or overruling the firm's risk controls on a regular basis. Delaware law sets a high bar for establishing a breach of the fiduciary duty of care. Basically, there was no evidence, based on Delaware law, that Lehman's senior management was irresponsible or unreasonable in managing the risks associated with the principal investment strategy that Lehman pursued during 2006 and 2007.

## 6.2 BCCI

The bankruptcy of the Bank of Credit and Commerce International (BCCI) is considered as one of the greatest financial disasters of the twentieth century. Founded in 1972 by a Pakistani banker the BCCI had an exponential growth, so much so that in 10 years, it became the seventh bank in the world for assets (20 billion dollars) with 400 branches and a presence in 78 countries. The financial disaster, sanctioned by the Luxembourg court with the declaration of insolvency in 1991, was gigantic with losses of ten billion dollars. The financial failure of the BCCI was peculiar in the history of bank failures as it develops in parallel with the development of the bank. "The fraudulent activities of the BCCI in fact were not isolated but systematic and were an integral part of the banking business."[9] The magnitude of loophole in internal and external controls (at all levels) makes the BCCI's bankruptcy a case study for corporate governance failure.

### *6.2.1 BCCI Foundation*[10]

The BCCI[11] was founded by the Pakistani banker Ali in 1972 with the participation in the capital of important strategic partners.[12] An important American bank contributed to the birth of the BCCI by financing 25% of the capital while an influential Abu Dhabi official, contributed both through the capital and through half of the initial deposits.[13] A lot of literature has been written on this scandal, but the reports commissioned by few central banks after the scandal blow up are the most insightful.

Ali's financial background dates to the 1960s when he created United Bank (UB) in Pakistan, which in a few years, thanks to Ali's commercial and political skills, became the second largest bank in the country. The Pakistani government's

[9] Bank of Credit and Commerce International Sa v. Ali and Others. Court of Appeal CA.

[10] BCCI internal document: Growth of International Banking, Case Study of Bank of Credit and Commerce Intl, Khruso Karamat Elley, October 27, 1982; Senate investigation.

Chossudovsky, Michel (5 April 2004). "The Spoils of War: Afghanistan's Multibillion Dollar Heroin Trade". Centre for Research on Globalization. Retrieved 5 August 2013.

Euromoney: "The Mysteries Behind Abedi's Bank" July 1978; S. Hrg. 103–350, Pt. 3, pp. 305–310.

House of Commons (1992). "Inquiry into the Supervision of The Bank of Credit and Commerce International".

Kanas, Angelos, "Pure contagion effects in International Banking: the case of BCCI's Failure". Journal of Applied Economics, Sunday, 1 May 2005.

Kerry, John; Hank Brown (December 1992). "The BCCI Affair: A Report to the Committee on Foreign Relations, United States Senate". 102d Congress 2d Session Senate.

Najam Sethi, "BCCI Founder: These Things Happen," Wall Street Journal, July 29, 1991.

Peter Truell, Larry Gurwin, False Profits. The Inside Story of BCCI, the world's most corrupt financial Empire, 1992, Houghton, Mifflin Company, Boston, New York, ISBN 0-395-62339-1.

RA Barnes Esq: Report on Sandstorm SA under section 41 of the Banking act 1987.

Nikos Passas. The Genesis of the BCCI Scandal. Journal of Law and Society. Vol. 23, No. 1, The Corruption of Politics, and the Politics of Corruption (Mar., 1996), pp. 57–72.

[11] Alford. "Core Principles for effective Banking Supervision: an enforceable international financial standard?" Boston College International and Comparative Law Review. 2005.

[12] Khruso Karamat Elley. Growth of International Banking: Case Study of Bank of Credit and Commerce Intl, October 27, 1982, Senate Document 385.

[13] Nikos Passas. The Genesis of the BCCI Scandal. Journal of Law and Society. Vol. 23, No. 1, The Corruption of Politics, and the Politics of Corruption (Mar., 1996), pp. 57–72 (16 pages).

decision in the early 1970s to nationalize the country's banks and major industries gave the final impetus to Ali's plan to internationalize the United Bank supported by the Abu Dhabi official and the American Bank. Ali's relationship with the Abu Dhabi official began in 1966 when Ali went to Abu Dhabi to request authorization to open a branch of the UB. The branch had an important commercial purpose as it represented for the many Pakistani workers in Abu Dhabi the possibility of being able to channel their savings home. Ali succeeded in transforming a simple commercial operation into an event of historical significance. The relationship between Ali and the Abu Dhabi official becomes so close that the investigation by the English House of Commons into the BCCI scandal traces the geopolitical vision that led to the creation of the UAE back to Ali.[14] Ali's political sensitivity was such that the Abu Dhabi officials, in search of international political legitimacy, used it as a diplomatic card in the world. The relationship with the American bank was instead based on characteristics of mere opportunism on both sides.[15] Ali needed an international bank that could guarantee and legitimize the name of Ali in the western banking elite, while for the American bank, the BCCI represented a potential entry into the rich world of the Middle East. Ali's first choice had been the American Express, but the latter's willingness to participate in the governance of BCCI tipped the balance in favor of the American bank which limited itself to requesting a silent stake in BCCI's capital. The American bank withdrew from the bankruptcy of the BCCI in time and sold its shares in 1980, but inevitably its reputation at the time suffered.

### *6.2.2 The Structure of the BCCI*

The initial capital of the BCCI for 2.5 million dollars was subscribed by the American bank while for 500,000 dollars by the Abu Dhabi official. The shareholding structure saw Ali with control of 50.1%, the American bank with 25%, and the Abu Dhabi official and other family members with the remaining shares. The Abu Dhabi official also deposited an initial $50 million which represented half of the deposits with which the BCCI started its business. The management of the BCCI was completely Pakistani and linked to Ali. Despite this apparent simplicity and linearity of the shareholding and managerial structure, the undergrowth that characterized the activity of BCCI was dense and full of incredible intertwining. BCCI was in fact controlled by a Luxembourg holding company (ICIC (Industrial Credit and Investment Corporation of India) holdings) which controlled the ICIC Oversee which held majority shares in BCCI. BCCI had registered offices in Luxembourg

[14]House of Commons (1992): Inquiry into the Supervision of The Bank of Credit and Commerce International.

[15]See, e.g "The Mysteries Behind Abedi's Bank," Euromoney July 1978; S. Hrg. 102–350 Pt. 3, pp. 305–310; "The man who adds a touch of mysticism to banking," Financial Times, May 17, 1978; S. Hrg. 102–350 Pt. 3, pp. 303–304.

and Grand Cayman. However, in Luxembourg, the BCCI did not carry out banking activities and therefore was not supervised by any supervisory authority, while in the Cayman, it enjoyed complete freedom as there were no supervisors. For each of the two registered offices, the BCCI had different auditors) who had no global vision of the BCCI's activity. Basically, at least in the early years of its activity, the BCCI enjoyed complete freedom without supervisors and with extremely limited auditing activity. However, the BCCI wanted to expand into the rich markets of Great Britain and the United States and succeeded during the 1970s and early 1980s.

### *6.2.3 The Structure of the Fraud*

The fraud from an accounting's point of view was generated since the establishment of the BCCI with the decision to create a bank with surreptitious capital.[16] In fact, part of the capital recorded had not actually been deposited, while another part of it contained hidden clauses for buybacks or guaranteed returns. In 1988, the main auditor[17] learned that 7.5% of the bank in the hands of a single shareholder was hiding a put option (a right to sell) against the controlling holding of BCCI. Many of the subsequent capital increases that followed were financed by the BCCI itself with loans to mysterious names. BCCI financed fictitious names with the deposits of its account holders to which it accounted for loans which were then used to underwrite the capital increases.

The "Sandstorm" document,[18] the Price Waterhouse secret report submitted to the Bank of England, showing that the Bank of Credit and Commerce International (BCCI) had engaged in widespread fraud, showed that 8 of the 15 members of the BCCI board were fictitious names. Fifty-eight percent of the capital of the BCCI was directly financed by the BCCI itself with loans of $1.4 billion. Another characteristic of the BCCI capital was that it was financed with undistributed profits never realized. The report notes that as of June 1985, 850 million dollars in profits made by the BCCI were fictitious. In particular, the interest margin contained revenues deriving from nonperforming loans that were accounted for but never collected, while trading commissions contained fictitious collections on transactions that were never carried out.

Another incredible accounting aspect that leaves astonished in the history of the BCCI is how the deposits of the millions of account holders were treated. The

---

[16] Kerry, John; Hank Brown (December 1992). "The BCCI Affair: A Report to the Committee on Foreign Relations, United States Senate". 102d Congress 2d Session Senate.

[17] Price Waterhouse audit reports to BCCI board of directors, 1987–1989; miscellaneous BCCI loan and financial documents (part of the John Kerry Report).

[18] RA Barnes Esq: Report on Sandstorm SA under section 41 of the Banking act 1987.

management of the BCCI used the deposits of the account holders as a sort of ATM with which it financed current expenses. This is a real description of our second agency cost (depositors vs shareholders and directors).

In the books of the BCCI, according to the report by Senator Kerry, there were loans to auditors, to employees, and to many politicians and strategic figures (see Footnote 16). In 1987, the main auditor revealed that among the BCCI's largest clients, with loans amounting to 200 million dollars, was the former head of Saudi Arabian intelligence. Price Waterhouse points out in his report that the loan was not covered by guarantees and that it was remunerated with extremely advantageous interest rates (see Footnote 17). In 1978, the American authorities had already reported anomalous situations in the BCCI's accounting books with an exposure to a single Arab group equal to double the bank's capital. In the context of the scams orchestrated by the BCCI over the years, the subsidiary CapCom plays a leading role.

### 6.2.4 The Capcom System: The BCCI Laundry

Senator Kerry's report (1992) to the US Congress very accurately describes CapCom's business. CapCom was founded in 1984 in London by former BCCI treasurer (see Footnote 16). BCCI controlled the capital. In a short time, CapCom became one of the leading brokers for trading on commodities in London and consequently in the world. Owning a commodity, broker was strategically perfect for the BCCI which uses it to structure complex money laundering operations. The diabolical beauty of CapCom was that being a broker, it did not have a supervision comparable to that of a bank but above all it could operate on very high volumes through futures (forward contracts). This made it very easy to disguise illegal transactions. CapCom's illegal operations were structured through mirror operations that consisted of the purchase and sale of forward contracts for the same account but marked by different contract names. This operation made it possible to clean up the profits and losses of the operations as they flowed into the income statement of the same account with the opposite sign. These trades were lost among myriads of truthful commodity trades and left no trace. What appeared to be transactions between two accounts were simple transfers of funds between two accounts of the same individual. Thus, money of dubious origin was transformed into brokerage commissions, bank deposits, and capital market operations.

### 6.2.5 Beginning of the Problem

During the 1970s, there were many anonymous letters and various reports that the various regulators received on the activities of the BCCI.[19] However, it was only in 1979 that the Bank of England invited the BCCI to commission its auditing firm to inspect the bank's loan portfolio. The answer was, however, reassuring, although one of the auditors itself wrote to Ali-in 1980 raising strong doubts about internal controls and the quality of information.[20] The problem of the absence of a single auditor for the group who had a global view on BCCI was raised by both the Fed and the Bank of England. Ali, feeling encircled, decided to entrust the single overhaul to a unique auditing company in 1987.[21]

In the meantime, however, the rumors about the shady business of BCCI and the real solidity of the bank had spread to such an extent that 72 banks around the world were closing interbank credit lines. The defining episode that triggered the downward spiral of BCCI was the colossal loss of the London BCCI Treasury in 1985. An inexperienced junior trader, hired directly by Ali and immediately placed in charge of a billionaire desk, caused a monstrous loss of $500 million through reckless commodity trading. To try to mask the trading losses, the trader sold a huge number of forward contracts to collect the commissions and possibly postpone the problem.[22] In practice, the income statement in the short term was covered by commissions that masked trading losses while the potential issues of future contracts were postponed. In the fall of 1985, BCCI's futures (forward contracts) exposure in its London office had reached an astronomical figure of $11 billion against a limit granted by the BCCI's board of directors of $1 billion. The trader later to the magistrates told a very different story. He accused CEO of making up the commodity loss story to hide years of accounting tricks that could no longer be disguised.[23] Putting the blame on an unscrupulous and inexperienced trader could appear as an easy way out for the market, auditors, and controllers. Whatever the story went, the image of the BCCI and who was paid to control it fell apart. Hence, the need for BCCI and the trader to create CapCom (before the repudiation of his putative father—the CEO) is to continue its business through a new vehicle. Meanwhile, the situation for BCCI was also becoming explosive in the US subsidiary, where the main managers were arrested on charges of money laundering.

---

[19] Price Waterhouse, Draft Report on Sandstorm SA Under S. 41 of the Savings Act of 1987.

[20] https://www.nytimes.com/1991/09/16/business/auditing-the-auditors-a-special-report-how-bcci-s-accounts-won-stamp-of-approval.html

[21] Richard Dale. Reflections on the BCCI Affair: A United Kingdom Perspective. The International Lawyer 1992.

[22] Kerry, John; Hank Brown (December 1992). "The BCCI Affair: A Report to the Committee on Foreign Relations, United States Senate". 102d Congress 2d Session Senate. Pag 251.

[23] Kerry, John; Hank Brown (December 1992). "The BCCI Affair: A Report to the Committee on Foreign Relations, United States Senate". 102d Congress 2d Session Senate. Pag 252.

### 6.2.6 BCCI and the Entry in the US Market

The entry of the BCCI into the American banking market is worthy of a detective film. In the 1970s, the BCCI tried to enter the American banking market directly as the relationship with the American bank in the United States had not borne the desired results. The BCCI first attempted to acquire another famous American bank directly and sought permission to open branches in New York. The Fed in both cases stopped Ali despite the powerful political support he could count on (see Footnote 16).

The Fed was particularly concerned about the absence of a primary supervisor for the BCCI as a group by the Bank of England, despite the BCCI's main business being in London, refused to perform this function as it considered the BCCI to be a foreign bank and therefore applied secondary supervision.[24] Despite the resistance of the FED, Ali and the BCCI managed not only to enter the US banking market but to acquire four banks. The system's device was very simple. In practice, Ali and the BCCI made loans to various nominees who acquired control of the acquired banks. All this is in total violation of US law. The American justice, unable to prove the violation directly as the figureheads were in the Middle East with no possibility of obtaining detailed information, somehow tried to attack the BCCI through CapCom. CapCom, unlike BCCI, had entered the US market much more easily as a commodity broker, so it could trade on the Chicago Stock Exchange market freely. In 1988, the US Department of Justice succeeded in indicting and convicting the top managers of CapCom for money laundering. The trader, who became CEO of CapCom, was arrested in London where he was sentenced to 18 months in prison. The media's impact in the United States and Great Britain was high, and there were fears for a possible leak of deposits. However, the monitoring of liquidity ordered by the Bank of England did not report large deposit losses thanks to the excellent media defense that Ali and the BCCI managed to organize. However, it was clear that, albeit in evident delay, the attention of supervisors toward the BCCI was destined to increase significantly. Meanwhile, during 1988, Ali was hospitalized for two heart attacks and was diagnosed with serious neurological damage. From that moment, the control of the BCCI passed into the hands of the historic number two of the BCCI, Naqvi. And the situation worsened. The attitude of the auditors changes radically. In 1990, the auditing company warned the Bank of England that there were significant accounting problems in the BCCI's balance sheets and that there was evidence of fraud. The Bank of England and the auditor immediately understood that the situation could become explosive. They then decided to start a questionable hidden rescue operation.

In practice, negotiations were opened with the important Abu Dhabi official to "convince him" to take control of the bank and inject the liquidity and capital

---

[24] Jonathan Beaty, S. C. Gwynne The Outlaw Bank: A Wild Ride Into the Secret Heart of BCCI Paperback – February 1, 2004.

necessary to save it in exchange for maintaining the activity of the same and in exchange for the promise by the auditing company to certify the financial statements of the BCCI. The Bank of England itself allowed the transfer of the BCCI headquarters from London to Abu Dhabi in 1990. The report by US Senator Kerry on the *BCCI Affair* presented to the Senate in 1992 highlights how this was a very serious mistake on the part of the Bank of England as it significantly limited the investigation into the case and the possibility for the victims of the scam, to be able to obtain justice and compensation. In 1991, the Bank of England commissioned the BCCI auditors to carry out a thorough and secret inspection of the BCCI accounts whose long-secret report was called "Sandstorm." The report, which today can be found on the Internet through the WikiLeaks website, contains the true dimensions of the BCCI's financial hole.[25] The report highlighted how 600 million deposits had completely disappeared in the coffers of BCCI in the 1990 balance sheet; 58% of the BCCI capital had been financed directly by the BCCI itself through 1.4 billion dollars in loans to eight different shareholders. The latter also received substantial commissions by virtue of their service. The report estimates that approximately 22 million dollars were paid to nominee shareholders for their service. It was pointed out that a whopping 850 million dollars in false profit had accumulated since 1985. The bill for the Abu Dhabi government to save the BCCI was huge. Abu Dhabi decided to create a fund of 1.7 billion dollars to partially repay the defrauded account holders who, in any case, had to be satisfied with receiving 30% of the initial sums. Another $5.2 billion was spent on filling accounting holes and on recapitalizing the bank and taking control of it. The agreement with the liquidators allowed the Abu Dhabi government to close all possible claims for compensation for its role in the past in the BCCI affair.

### 6.2.7 The Role of Ali

To fully understand the history of the BCCI and one of the most incredible financial frauds in history, it is necessary to analyze the figure of its deus ex machina, its Chairman Ali. The report of the investigation by the English House of Commons shows a portrait of Ali that is not too flattering.[26] Ali is described as an arrogant man with a huge ego. Ali "has combined his defense of the poor and oppressed with a personal life of flamboyant opulence and a boundless ambition for power" (see Footnote 26). Senator Kerry's report to the US Congress underlines a different, and certainly decisive, aspect of Ali's personality: the great charisma that Ali exercised. The charisma and personality of Ali were the glue of the BCCI so much so that,

[25] https://www.wikileaks.com/wiki/BCCI_Sandstorm_report,_1991

[26] House of Commons (1992): Inquiry into the Supervision of The Bank of Credit and Commerce International.

following the departure of Ali from the management of the Bank due to the heart crisis and the loss of neurological functions in 1988, the BCCI collapsed.

Here is how the report to the congress reports the description of Ali by former BCCI finance director Maxim Ram, who worked alongside Ali for nearly two decades, "Ali was a man whose personality dominated all those around him, who could transform great personalities into saints or devils at the same time. I remember looking Ali in the eye and seeing God and the Devil equally balanced in them. He was already an older man when he started BCCI, and he was determined not to waste time taking his vision and turning it into something very big. Ali demanded the total devotion of everyone around him. If one of his employees decided to abandon an Ali project, he considered it a personal disgrace ... ... For example, when an important BCCI manager received two offers from other banks and decided to leave BCCI, Ali refused to accept the situation."[27]

The manager thus describes the scene of his resignation in front of Ali. "I told Ali I had to leave. He told me that clearly, I could do what I wanted, but he begged me to stay and that he would not let me go. I said: Mr. Ali things are getting very difficult. I have two offers, one from Citicorp and one from BOP Canada. He started to cry. It was heart-breaking . . .. . . We are people from the East, who are not trained to handle such things. I said: Mr. Ali, my fate is in your hands, and I decided to stay."[28]

Ali's charisma was such that BCCI's corporate culture fully reflected Ali's personality. During company meetings, Ali could talk for hours about the culture of BCCI and the philosophy behind its growth. Ali's philosophy was described as a mixture of Islamic mysticism that focused on the bonds between the individual and the family.[29] Here is how Ali described it: "Our organization has its own meaning that emerges far from our needs, our objectives, our quality and the quantity of human resources .... We accept the truth that each of us is different and like every being human, each of us is inadequate, but unlike others, we must truly accept the other and have a huge need and desire to constantly move towards adequacy. . . The quality of relationships has it. . . it is the essence of our organization. It is the shining truth. It is the truth that every single member of our family must reveal in their feelings - in their psyche. It must arouse like a bright star in its heart". . . .. . . "We must learn that the BCCI is the POWER, it is not a simple group of branches or numbers . . .. . . this is the will of GOD" (see Footnote 29).

Ali's philosophy fully described the need for the bank's ongoing pursuit of growth. It was God's will and had to be pursued at any cost. That is why the managers of the BCCI who were sanctioned by the local supervisory authorities for misconduct were not fired by the BCCI but were simply transferred to another country.

---

[27] Staff interview, Rahman, August 7, 1991. Kerry, John Report.

[28] Staff interview, Sakhia, October 7, 1991.

[29] "Context and Rationale," Statement of Agha Hasan Abedi to BCCI officials, undated, Senate BCCI Document 1269.

Another pillar of Ali's philosophy was the strategy, inherited from the secret services, of keeping information separated by sector. In practice, this ensured that no one within the BCCI had a complete picture of the situation, except him and his deputy. The BCCI from an organizational point of view was structured without a real top management (except Ali and his deputy). Figures such as the vice presidents were completely absent, replaced by 52 senior executives and 198 managers. However, none of them had full access to all the BCCI information. The directors of the Board of Directors were defined RAF,[30] "rent a face." Ali essentially "rented" people to fully support its management.

### 6.2.8 *The Other BCCI's Activities*

According to Senator Kerry's report to the American Senate, BCCI's activities were extremely diversified into other strategic sectors of organized crime, so much so that the congressional report defines it as the largest organized crime case in history, branching into 72 countries with around 3000 clients, belonging to crime. The report talks about the involvement of the BCCI in arms, drug, and other trafficking (see Footnote 30), all to finance the growth of the BCCI by any means. It is no coincidence that the BCCI was the international bank par excellence with an extremely extensive network with the ability to open all the doors of world politics.

Through coordinated action, on July 5, 1991, eight national regulators decided to close the BCCI branches present in their countries (see Footnote 11). The closures followed one another for several days, and on July 29, 1991, 45 of the 74 countries in which the BCCI was active decided to withdraw their banking license and closed the local branches. In the same year, the liquidators of the BCCI, after having decreed the state of insolvency, began their legal battle, which ended in nothing, against the Bank of England, held responsible for the financial disaster of the BCCI for not having exercised its duty of control as directed supervisor. The liquidators accused the Bank of England of causing £9 billion ($16 billion) losses. The Bank of England accused the liquidators of causing losses to citizens by virtue of the very high legal costs associated with the case (£100 million). The legal battle between the various parties ended only in 2012, 21 years later. The only winners were the lawyers and consultants who shared the beauty of 665 million dollars in fees to unravel the tangle of the most complex bank's insolvency case in history.[31]

---

[30] Inquiry into the Supervision of The Bank of Credit and Commerce International.

[31] http://hereisthecity.com/en-gb/2012/05/18/files-close-on-bcci-banking-scandal/

## 6.3 Bankhaus Herstatt

The bankruptcy of the German Bank Bankhaus Herstatt is considered, due to the ramifications of its impact, despite its small size, as the determining factor that prompted the central bank governors of the ten most industrialized countries to launch the Banking Supervision Committee (Basel Committee). Herstatt's failure provides an illustration of the consequences of poor oversight by the supervisors, poor internal governance, as well as the limitation of market self-regulation.[32]

### *6.3.1 Herstatt Affairs*

Herstatt Bank, which in 1974 had an honorable banking history of nearly 250 years, was a medium-sized financial institution based in Cologne, Germany. Very active in currency trading, it had very significant international ramifications despite not being among the top 30 German banks in terms of asset size. The real protagonist of the Herstatt affair is undoubtedly the head of the trading room specializing in currency exchange trading, Daniel Wolf (who joined the bank as an intern in 1958. Wolf's childhood was peculiar, and his life seems marked since birth. Wolf was born in 1940, and at the age of 4, he found himself with his mother in the Auschwitz concentration camp in the labor section. After the war, he dreamed of becoming an actor, but he found himself studying finance, and after completing his studies, he was hired by the Herstatt Bank. His career proceeded smoothly, and Wolf was promoted to head of the FX (foreign exchange) desk.

### *6.3.2 The Red and Black of Wolf*

As Mourlon-Druol (2015a, b) pointed out in his paper, the origin of the Herstatt disaster was routed in the bad governance and "the relaxed attitude of Ivan Herst (major shareholder of the Bank with 81.4% of shares) towards his bank's foreign currency division." Mr. Herst decided to trust completely the senior management capacity to handle the riskier part of its bank assets. Ivan Herst clearly knew very little about what was going on in his own bank, and the German supervisors complained about it several times.[33] Herst wrote in his memoirs that he assigned the responsibility to supervise the foreign currency dealings to the general

[32]Emmanuel Mourlon-Druol 'Trust is good, control is better': 2015 The 1974 Herstatt Bank Crisis and its Implications for International Regulatory Reform Adam Smith Business School, University of Glasgow, Glasgow, UK https://www.tandfonline.com/doi/full/10.1080/00076791.2014.950956.

[33]Mourlon-Druol, E. 'Trust is good, control is better': the 1974 Herstatt-Bank crisis and its implications for international regulatory reform. (Business History 2015).

representative of the bank Von der Goals, as he was too busy on other responsibilities (see Footnote 34).

Year 1973 was a pivotal year in Wolf's life and career. Wolf believed that the dollar was overvalued and decided to bet against the fixed exchange rate of the mark for the dollar and the dollar for gold. The dollar which enjoyed a fixed exchange rate with gold at 44 dollars an ounce traded on the secondary market at 70 dollars an ounce. Wolf was convinced that the dollar would devalue because of a possible decision by the Fed to unpeg it from gold. Wolf, with the full support of the board that had approved the risk limits, built a short position on the dollar against the German Deutsche Mark. The idea behind the operation was that sooner or later, the US government could unpeg the dollar from gold and leave it free to float. In fact, in the summer of 1971, growing speculation forced convertibility to be suspended for a few weeks. In 1972, the pound was the first to break away from the fixed exchange rate regime. In March 1973, the Japanese Yen followed the same fate against the American currency. After a few days, Nixon announced the decision to abandon the gold standard. The exchange underwent an extremely high volatility, so much so that from February to July 1973, the US dollar fell from a rate of 2.97 against the DM, devaluing by 23%. By February 1973, Wolf had sold $1 billion for a value of DM 3 billion. In May 1973, Wolf closed his short position with a gain of $500 million. One billion dollars was worth 2.5 billion German Deutsche Mark. Wolf and his team became superstars and soon their autonomy became total. The bank and the council practically gave him carte blanche.

The foreign exchange market in the meantime had become one of the most liquid with the participation of all the major world banks. US banks were the most present and aggressive on this market. Their presence on the London market had tripled in a few years with assets outside the United States that had gone from 6% of the total to 14%. The offshore foreign exchange business in London was a ground with very light oversight. To help the lack of transparency and the dangerousness of the sector contributed to the emergence in those years of offshore financial centers such as the Cayman Islands, Guernsey, and Nassau, which offered fertile ground to banks "allergic" to supervision. In those years, the ideal conditions had been created to create enormous positions without controls.

### 6.3.3 *The Second Bet*

In September of the same year, Wolf and his team decided to try a new trade again. The Currency Trading Department was made up of six very young traders of which Wolf was in charge. Each of them had a daily limit of $10 million. Even with maximum exhaustion, the volume of trade should not have exceeded $15 billion per year—about 40 billion Deutsche Mark, depending on the exchange rate.

Wolf decided to bet again in the same direction as the previous trade. Wolf's team built a huge deutsche mark versus dollar position. This time the trade did not work.

The US monetary policy and the oil crisis led the US dollar to recover, and in February 1974, the dollar returned to 2.76 against the deutsche mark.

However, Wolf decided not to disclose the accumulated losses to the bank's internal controls and instead accumulated new positions against the dollar to be able to lower the carrying price of his position.

In the meantime, the rumors regarding the losses of Wolf and his team became more and more insistent, and soon the internal controls asked for explanations.[34] As Mourlon-Druol (2015a, b) pointed out in his paper, "Herstatt had been building a negative reputation from 1971 at least, but somehow some market actors and regulators overlooked the origins of this reputation and carried on dealing with the German bank regardless."

Wolf tried to mask the losses again by saying that the positions were all neutralized (hedged) and that therefore the losses highlighted by the trades were offset by favorable positions on the hedges. Only in February 1974, the German supervisors of BAKred began an inspection at the FX trading rooms of the Bank Herstatt.[35] The FX trading rooms at that time were composed by six active traders with operations that were registered daily in a computer. The Karoli Wirtschaftsprüfung concluded from this survey: "We consider the current technical organization as sufficient to process the volume of transactions."

Mourlon-Druol (2015a, b) pointed out that "what the Karoli Wirthschaftsprüfung did not find out, however, was the existence of a 'cancel button' (Abbruchtaste)." Using this button allowed the trader's operations not to appear in the daily list of operations carried out by the bank, printed out by the computer. Herstatt explains that Wolf could use this cancel button and could thus manipulate the daily balance sheets. According to Der Spiegel, this function had been used increasingly frequently since early 1973.[36] Mourlon-Druol (2015a, b) mentions that "Herstatt adds in his memoirs that he has subsequently found that Herr Wolf occasionally exceeded his limit up to 750 million."

In May and June 1974, market rumors about the real Herstatt financial situation were so spread that some banks refused to trade with Herstatt.[37]

It was only on June 10, 1974, when the situation started to become unmanageable that Ivan Herst started to become aware of the first significant losses.[38] Von der Goals revealed that day to Herstatt that "we have been lied to and suffered around 100 million losses in currency trading in the current year." However, the reality was even worst that initially depicted. The supervisors found unhedged positions of $3.2

[34] BAK, B 126/59463, Note of Stauch, Betreff: Bankhaus I.D. Herstatt KG a.A., Köln, 12 July 1973.

[35] BAK, B 126/59463, Stauch (Bundesaufsichtsamt für das Kreditwesen) to the Karoli Wirtschaftsprüfung GmBH, Jahresabschlussprüfung beim Bankhaus I.D. Herstatt KGaA, Köln, 25 February 1974.

[36] Gespielt, getäuscht, gemogelt: Die Anatomie der Herstatt-Pleite,' Der Spiegel, 31 March 1975.

[37] Goodhart, The Basel Committee on Banking Supervision, chapter 5.

[38] BoE, 3A49/2, I.D. Herstatt, 4 July 1974.

billion versus deutsche mark 8 billion. The uncovered position was equal to four times the capital of the Bank Herstatt. The losses were unknown to Wolf himself who declared three different losses to the supervisory authority in a few days. He started with the manageable figure of 25 million in losses to go from 208 million in losses to the monster figure of 480 million dollars.[39] In practice, considering the underlying losses, the bank was insolvent.

The German supervisor tried to remedy the situation by contacting the three major German banks trying to persuade them, unsuccessfully, to acquire the trades of the Herstatt Bank.

### *6.3.4 The Timing for the Bank Resolution*

The regulators decided to decree the state of insolvency and to close the Bank Herstatt on June 26, 1974, on Wednesday. The timing was nefarious. It was chosen a Wednesday and not, as normally in this crisis situations, on Friday with closed markets to have 2 days to manage the crisis. Moreover, the bank's resolution took place at the end of the working day in Frankfurt, which was the morning of a working day in New York, thus leaving a certain number of open operations. This generated the so-called Herstatt risk (settlement risk), that is, the risk taken by carrying out transactions in different time zones. The chosen date, according to some historians, had its own logic. It was the day when the German national football team would be involved in a match, valid for the football World Cup, against Yugoslavia. Supervisor likely believed that the game could limit the negative effects of the news of the closure of the Bank Herstatt. Many German traders probably would not have been on their desks but at the bar enjoying the game, and probably there would have been no rush to the bank as the account holders would have been distracted by the event. However, the authorities had greatly underestimated the impacts. While Herstatt was an only relatively small banking player in the German market, the effects for the international banking system were significant due to the negative shock in corresponding banking operations. The financial disaster generated by the unfortunate choice of timing led to huge losses resulting from the failure to settle currency transactions. Particularly during the German business day of June 26, some of Herstatt's banking counterparties had irrevocably paid significant amounts of deutsche mark to the bank. However, due to the time difference with the US financial market that had just opened, they had not yet received any dollars in exchange. The decision of the German authorities to declare bankruptcy and closure of the bank thus gave way to a chain reaction that interrupted international payment systems. The banks that had made payments in deutsche mark to the Bank Herstatt

[39] BAK, B126/59464, Note of Reuther, Zeitplan über Einflussnahmen des BAKred auf die Herstatt-Bank, 20 August 1974. These elements have been reported by Weiler at a meeting at LBZ in Düsseldorf on 23 June 1974.

that day found themselves uncovered in the corresponding dollar counterpart of these transactions. Twelve banks had sent Bankhaus Herstatt $620 million worth of marks becoming de facto its unsecured creditors.

After 9 years of investigation and several trials, in 1983, several managers involved in the disaster were convicted of fraud. Wolf was never imprisoned as following the story he gave signs of mental imbalance which were diagnosed as symptoms of KZ. The coroners traced the origin of the disease to his childhood and the time spent in the concentration camp of Auschwitz. By the end of June 1984, all the crimes charged had expired when he asked the cologne regulatory office to get his driver's license back. The document had been withdrawn 5 years earlier because Dany was under severe psychotropic influence from psychotropic drugs due to a mental illness ("concentration camp syndrome").

Among the few positive notes of the Herstatt Bank's unfortunate handling of the financial crisis was that it was the determining factor that prompted the central bank governors of the ten most industrialized countries to launch the Banking Supervision Committee (Basel Committee). It was set up at the end of 1974 to institute simultaneous or quasi-simultaneous settlement of foreign currency payments and limit the temporal risk (which from then on took the name of risk Herstatt). According to a paper published by ECB[40] "the Herstatt case demonstrated very clearly how risky the lack of synchronism between the settlement of the two legs of a foreign exchange. "Herstatt risk", as it has come to be known, is a type of risk that payment systems had not been, and for a long time afterwards were still not, designed to cope with adequately. In the mid-1990s, the Basel-based Committee on Payment and Settlement Systems (CPSS) created a sub-group to investigate potential solutions to the issue, and a risk-reduction strategy to eliminate foreign exchange (FX) settlement risk was subsequently agreed upon by G10 central banks."[41]

From a corporate governance point of view, the Herstatt case is an excellent example of what bad governance could bring at. Babiak and Hare[42] in their studies on corporate psychopaths found that the incident of psychopath with senior positions in corporates is four times higher than the normal population. Lack of board oversight on management activity combined to a lack of effective supervision by the competent authorities and a lack of market self-regulation brought a little German bank to paralyze payments systems around the world for several days.

[40]https://www.ecb.europa.eu/pub/financial-stability/fsr/focus/2007/pdf

[41]CPSS (1996), "Settlement Risk in Foreign Exchange Transactions", BIS, March.

[42]Robert D. Hare, Ph.D. and Paul Babiak, Ph.D., authors of "Snakes in Suits: When Psychopaths Go to Work" ACFE Bookstore.

## 6.4 Societe Generale: Rogue Traders

Herstatt case was, among other things, an example of the consequences of how a trader left without a proper supervision could bring to. This case was not unique, and in the recent years, numerous other similar events happened. We will investigate in this chapter two other famous examples.

On January 24, 2008, the Societe Generale General Inspection department was entrusted by the bank to carry out an investigation concerning the Daniel Kerit activity (we use a fictitious name).[43] The purpose of the investigation was, among others, to describe the mechanism used to perpetrate the fraud and to identify the malfunctioning of control procedures and responsibility for the late detection of the fraud. The results revealed several shortcomings from a governance point of view. Just 3 years after the Kerit scandal, a very similar incident hit UBS's credibility. The aim of this chapter is not to describe the frauds per se but rather highlights the governance holes described by the investigations.

### *6.4.1 Societe Generale Derivatives Affair*

Francois Brochet (2009)[44] wrote that the Societe Generale case illustrates the tension/balance that firms with complex and risky business models must consider in designing their internal controls. It describes the environment in which a derivatives trader engaged in massive directional positions on major European stocks and indexes without being detected for over a year.

Kerit joined SG in 2000 working in the back offices while moving in 2005 to front office as junior trader. The main Kerit's activity was supposed to be focused on exploiting arbitrage position (as securities listed in different countries with different prices). Usually profits on this kind of activity can be only marginal. To increase his profits, according to the Mission Green Report (2008), for the desk, Kerit started first taking unauthorized positions in shares of Allianz and then in options, futures, and forwards in addition to equities. "Between 2006 and 2007, Kerit's earnings were multiplied by 6, growing to represent 59% of the earnings of DELTA ONE desk Listed Products."[45] After some initial gains, he started, according to the Mission Green Report (2008), also accumulating losses. To show a stable level of profits, he used a parallel accounting building opposite trades to the real one to avoid limits and controls. In July 2007, he accumulated $42 billion short positions in DAX (***Deutscher Aktienindex***) futures while changing in 2008 to a long position on

---

[43] https://www.societegenerale.com/en/news/newsroom/kerviel-case

[44] Brochet, Francois. "Societe Generale (A): The Jerome Kerviel Affair." Harvard Business School Case 110-029, October 2009. (Revised April 2010).

[45] Mission Green Report. (2008). General inspection analysis.

index futures (unhedged) for $72 billion. The position was discovered on January 20, 2008.

A young auditor found that one of his positions was unhedged contrary to what Kerit has declared. Kerit explained, according to the Mission Green Report (2008), that the trades were canceled 1 week before. On Friday, January 18, Kerit explained that he booked wrongly the name of the counterparties for the trade and provided the name of a US counterparty. Auditor called him and discovered that it was not true. The house of cards was finally dismantled.

The size of the position, not hedged, put the bank at risk, so it was decided to unwind it. On January 24, 2008, the Societe Generale reported loss for ca€5.8 billion due to "exceptional fraudulent trading activities."

Societe Generale General Inspection's investigation reports focus on the internal control's failure and the dynamics of the fraud. The Mission Green's report highlights three main techniques used by Kerit to conceal his fraudulent directional positions.

The first type of technique (counted in 947 transactions) was based on recording fictitious trades. To hide losses or gain, Kerit entered one or several false transactions into the systems so that they would be considered in risk and valuation calculations (hedging the real exposure). These transactions combined two main characteristics as follows:

*- a significant offset (i.e. the difference between the transaction date and the 30-day order value date) and a cancellation before the value date;*

*- the use of internal counterparties within the SG Group or small-scale external counterparties with cancellation before the value date in all cases.*

The controls bypassed thanks to these transactions were the following:

*- No settlement or delivery due to the cancellation of the transactions.*

*- No confirmation until 5 days before the value date for transactions with a deferred value date.*

*- No confirmation for internal transactions as these is reviewed in the context of intra-group transactions.*

*- No margin calls with small counterparties that do not have any collateralization agreements (only limits or "independent amount").*

The second type of technique (counted in 115 transactions) was based on setting fictitious transactions that matched each other in the inverse.

Kerit entered these equal quantities fictitious reverse transactions (purchase/sale of the same asset) for different "off-market" prices to match the realized earnings without creating a directional position. These transactions combined the following main characteristics:

*- a significant offset (i.e. difference between the transaction date and the 30 days value date) and cancellation before the value date;*

*- use of internal SG group counterparties or of small-scale counterparties with cancellation before the value date in all cases.*

The controls bypassed, thanks to these transactions, were like the one described before: no settlements and no confirmation due to the cancelation. At the same time, there were no margin calls with small counterparties since they do not have any collateralization agreements.

The third type of technique (counted in nine transactions) was based on recording provision flow ("flux pro").

> Kerit used the option, in principle reserved for trading assistants (but without any technological protection preventing access by traders) to correct modelling bias, to enter positive or negative provisions modifying the value calculated by the Front Office system. He entered such flows to conceal the amount of earnings generated by his fraudulent positions. Kerit knew that they were only monitored at the end of the month and cancelled them before the control took place.

The report by the Societe Generale General Inspection department, called Mission Green, highlighted the following five major governance reasons why the bank failed to detect Kerit's activities:

1. Weaknesses of the supervision. The trading desk manager missed his two principal tasks in relation to control measures. He did not check that the desk's net position does not exceed the allocated risk limit, and he did not consult on a regular basis the tool explaining profits or losses made to monitor the activity of his traders. Supervisor's weakness materialized also versus signals coming from external sources. For at least two times in November 2007, Eurex sent inquiry concerning Kerit's activity, neglected by Kerit's direct hierarchical superior.
2. Staff risk, the inexperience of Kerit's manager and lack of experience and seniority in back/middle office teams, and the different status between the traders, considered as profit center, and the controllers viewed internally as cost center. "With the omnipresence of the profit culture, I perceived a hidden hierarchy between the 'cost centers' like the support functions—the back and middle office—and the 'profit centers', that is, the front office staff—the traders and the sales teams. Cost centers, profit centers, I couldn't say how many times I heard those words. They had entered everyone's language as well as the collective unconscious."[46]
3. Ineffective control systems particularly the tolerance given of the taking of intraday directional positions within the desk, created a context in which Kerit operated more freely.
4. Lack of sensitivity to the risk of fraud. Kerit's hierarchy, which never had any knowledge of either the size of the incriminated positions or the mechanisms used to conceal them, lacked responsiveness in the face of several signals. Kerit explains "in the trading room, the ideal modus operandi can be summed up in one sentence: knowing how to take risks to make the maximum amount of money for the bank. In the name of such a rule, the most basic principles of prudence do not carry much weight" (see Footnote 47).
5. Deteriorating operational situation rendered difficult by strong, rapid growth in the division. Clear signs were neglected such as doubling of volumes in

[46] J. Kerviel L'engrenage. Mémoires d'un trader Flammarion, Paris (2010).

12 months, Front Office employee numbers growing from 4 to 23 in 2 years, multiplication of the number of products, and Middle Office chronically understaffed in 2007 following numerous departures. Moreover, Kerit's reluctance to take any vacation, raised formally by the DELTA ONE manager on four occasions (in February 2007, November 2007, and during his 2006 and 2007 annual appraisals), without concrete effect, did not alert his hierarchical superiors.

## 6.5 UBS'S Scandal

Just three years after the Kerit scandal, a very similar incident hit UBS credibility. Abdel exploited his role as a trader at UBS in London, resulting in a financial loss for the bank of around $2.3 billion.[47]

The career of Abdel had some similarities with the Kervit one. At the beginning of his professional career at UBS as part of the back-office department, Kweku Abdel was able to gain detailed knowledge of both the trading systems and the risk and control systems. Then he was promoted to the front office and become a member of the DELTA ONE desk whose primary activity was arbitrage trading, which is based on proprietary trading and the generation of profits with a generally low net risk position.

The techniques used by Abdel to disguise positions which were more than his desk's net delta limits showed somehow some similarities to the one used by Kervit. The most prominent among them is referred to as "umbrella." This construct consisted of fake accounts into which fictitious trades were booked. The "umbrella" was used to hide profits from unhedged positions that could be utilized to cover potential losses. Other mechanisms, according to the investigation,[48] include fictitious unmatched internal future trades. The front office risk system allowed traders to book internal future trades to a generic internal counterparty without requiring a matching trade or identification of the internal counterparty.

Moreover, according to the UBS's internal investigation, he manipulated the timing of booking trades. Several times he booked genuine future trades with external counterparties too late to misreport the current risk exposure of the desk.

Similarly, to Jerome Kerit of the Societe Generale, he made use of the fact that some ETF (exchange-traded fund) trades took a long time between the order and the settlement. Thus, just before settlement has taken place, Abdel canceled the order generating fictitious exposure for the time between order and settlement.

However, the most interesting parallelism with the Kervit story is that after the SG accident, the risk control function of UBS undertook a review of the UBS processes to assess its exposure to losses as a result of unauthorized trading triggered

---

[47] http://www.fsa.gov.uk/static/pubs/final/ubs-ag.pdf

[48] UBS AG. (2012), Annual report 2011, https://www.ubs.com/global/en/investor-relations/financial-information/annual-reporting/ar-archive.html.

by what happened in SG. The results of that investigation were that the supervision lacked effective management information, the reporting in place was ineffective to identify abnormal trading patterns, there were issues in the internal corporate governance culture, and the complexity reached by some areas of business could hamper the internal controls. These alerts were not enough to avoid the disaster in 2011 following the unauthorized Abdel trades.

An independent investigation requested by FSA (Financial Service Authority) highlighted several deficiencies in the UBS control governance. The corporate culture *in primis*. The report mentioned that "there was a culture of helping the traders to clear breaks based on the explanations they provided as opposed to challenging the traders and questioning whether their explanations were correct. As such the primary focus appears to have been on driving efficiency as opposed to more control-based activities" (see Footnote 48).

Inadequate and not integrated IT system allowing trades to be booked to an internal counterparty (similar to the SG case) without effective risk management systems able to detect trades priced materially off-market.

Lack of supervision which allowed Abdel to raise his revenues by five times in just 1 year is a level much greater than the increase in the risk limits of the desk without any enquires by his desk's line manager.

From the compliance and internal audit point of view, the FAS investigation[49] highlighted the following:

(a) *UBS' compliance monitoring lacked depth and a robust risk assessment process. The monitoring had limited impact on identifying and improving the control framework.*
(b) *UBS' risk and compliance functions were perceived by the front office to own issues relating to risk and control, rather than responsibility and accountability being accepted by the front office and/or back office.*
(c) *Some significant recommendations from group internal audit reports relating to the international wealth management business were not implemented by management in a timely manner.*
(d) *Insufficient supervision and the inadequate control of certain activities within the international wealth management business, most notably FX trading as described above, made it harder to detect unauthorized activities on a timely basis.*

### 6.5.1 Lesson Learned from the SG and the UBS Cases

Given the similarities of the unauthorized trades' episodes, it is possible to draw some lesson learned from the Societe Generale and UBS cases. Firstly, the risk

[49] https://webarchive.nationalarchives.gov.uk/20130202080455/ http://www.fsa.gov.uk/static/pubs/final/ubs_ag.pdf

culture of the control function should be tested frequently to check if there is a proper understanding of the risk and there is a proper challenging culture that allows control function to properly execute their controls. Control function should have a proper recognition inside the organization not perceived, as in some cases, as cost function.

Full understanding of the business model of the trading desk should be monitored as ensuring that risk limits are respected and punished properly and timely. The key requirements to allow this monitoring are proper tools and IT system that generate timely alert and prevent these kinds of incidents. These episodes showed clearly that a trader with high number of amended trades and canceled trades should be monitored with high attention.

## References

Alford D (2005) Core principles for effective banking supervision: an enforceable international financial standard? Boston Coll Int Comp Law Rev

BAK B 126/59463, Stauch (Bundesaufsichtsamt für das Kreditwesen) to the Karoli Wirtschaftsprüfung GmBH, Jahresabschlussprüfung beim Bankhaus I.D. Herstatt KGaA, Köln, 25 February 1974

Bank of Credit and Commerce International (n.d.) Sa v. Ali and Others. Court of Appeal CA

Beaty J, Gwynne SC (2004) The outlaw bank: a wild ride into the secret heart of BCCI paperback

Brochet F (2009) Societe Generale (A): the Jerome Kerviel Affair. Harvard Business School Case 110-029 (revised April 2010)

Chossudovsky M (2004) The spoils of war: Afghanistan's multibillion dollar heroin trade. Centre for Research on Globalization. Accessed 5 Aug 2013

Dale R (1992) Reflections on the BCCI affair: a United Kingdom perspective. International Lawyer

Elley KK (1982a) BCCI internal document: growth of international banking, case study of bank of credit and commerce international; Senate investigation

Elley KK (1982b) Growth of international banking: case study of bank of credit and commerce international. Senate document 385

Euromoney: "The mysteries behind Abedi's Bank" July 1978; S. Hrg. 103–350, Pt. 3, pp 305–310

Gespielt, getäuscht, gemogelt: Die Anatomie der Herstatt-Pleite, Der Spiegel, 31 March 1975

Goodhart (n.d.) The Basel Committee on banking supervision, Chapter 5

Hare RD, Babiak P (2006) Snakes in suits: when psychopaths go to work. ACFE Bookstore. Harper Business, New York

House of Commons (1992) Inquiry into the supervision of the bank of credit and commerce international

Kanas A (2005) Pure contagion effects in international banking: the case of BCCI's failure. J Appl Econ

Kerry J, Brown H (1992) The BCCI affair: a report to the committee on foreign relations, United States Senate. In 102d congress 2d session senate

Kerviel L'engrenage J (2010) Mémoires d'un trader Flammarion, Paris

Lehman Brothers Holdings Inc (n.d.) Chapter 11: Proceedings examiner's report. https://web.stanford.edu/~jbulow/Lehmandocs/menu.html

Mission Green Report (2008) General inspection analysis

Mourlon-Druol E (2015a) Trust is good, control is better: 2015. The 1974 Herstatt Bank Crisis and its implications for international regulatory reform Adam Smith Business School, University of Glasgow, Glasgow, UK. https://www.tandfonline.com/doi/full/10.1080/00076791.2014.950956

Mourlon-Druol E (2015b) 'Trust is good, control is better': the 1974 Herstatt-Bank crisis and its implications for international regulatory reform. Business history

Passas N (1996) The genesis of the BCCI scandal. J Law Soc 23(1):57–72

Price Waterhouse audit reports to BCCI board of directors, 1987-1989; miscellaneous BCCI loan and financial documents (part of the John Kerry Report)

RA Barnes Esq: report on sandstorm SA under section 41 of the banking act 1987

Report of Anton R. Valukas, Examiner (2010) United States Bankruptcy Court, Southern District of New York, In re Lehman Brothers Holdings Inc., et al., Debtors. March 11

Sethi N BCCI founder: these things happen. Wall Street Journal, July 29, 1991

Truell P, Gurwin L (1992) False profits. The inside story of BCCI, the world's most corrupt financial Empire. Houghton Mifflin Company, Boston. ISBN 0-395-62339-1

UBS AG (2012) Annual report 2011. https://www.ubs.com/global/en/investor-relations/financial-information/annual-reporting/ar-archive.html

# Correction to: Corporate Governance in the Banking Sector

## Correction to:
## B. Buchetti, A. Santoni, *Corporate Governance in the Banking Sector*, Contributions to Finance and Accounting, https://doi.org/10.1007/978-3-030-97575-3

This book was inadvertently published without updating the following corrections:

The city name "Pauda" has been replaced with "Padua."

The title of chapter 6 has been changed to "Why Corporate Governance Matters: Spectacular Defaults."

On page 143, section 6.2.1, the word "Abedi's" has been changed to "Ali's" in the second paragraph.

---

The updated online version of the book can be found at
https://doi.org/10.1007/978-3-030-97575-3
https://doi.org/10.1007/978-3-030-97575-3_6



B. Buchetti, A. Santoni, *Corporate Governance in the Banking Sector*, Contributions to Finance and Accounting, https://doi.org/10.1007/978-3-030-97575-3_7

The manufacturer's authorised representative in the EU is Springer
Nature Customer Service Centre GmbH, Europaplatz 3, 69115 Heidelberg,
Germany. If you have any concerns regarding our products, please
contact ProductSafety@springernature.com

Printed and bound by CPI Group (UK) Ltd, Croydon, CR0 4YY
24/09/2026
02222084-0001